THE PELICAN SHAKESPEARE
GENERAL EDITOR : ALFRED HARBAGE
AB19
ROMEO AND JULIET

WILLIAM SHAKESPEARE

The Tragedy of
Romeo and Juliet

EDITED BY JOHN E. HANKINS

PENGUIN BOOKS

BALTIMORE · MARYLAND

This edition first published 1960
Reprinted 1961
PENGUIN BOOKS INC.
3300 Clipper Mill Road, Baltimore 11, Maryland

[*Educational Representative: D. C. Heath & Co.
285 Columbus Avenue, Boston 16, Mass.*]

Printed in the United States of America

CONTENTS

SHAKESPEARE AND HIS STAGE

William Shakespeare was christened in Holy Trinity Church, Stratford-on-Avon, April 26, 1564. His birth is traditionally assigned to April 23rd. He was the eldest of four boys and two girls who survived infancy in the family of John Shakespeare, glover and trader of Henley Street, and his wife Mary Arden, daughter of a small landowner of Wilmcote. In 1568 John was elected Bailiff (equivalent to Mayor) of Stratford, having already filled the minor municipal offices. The town maintained for the sons of the burgesses a free school, taught by a university graduate and offering preparation in Latin sufficient for university entrance; its early registers are lost, but there can be little doubt that Shakespeare received the formal part of his education in this school.

On November 27, 1582, a license was issued for the marriage of William Shakespeare (aged eighteen) and Ann Hathaway (aged twenty-six), and on May 26, 1583, their child Susanna was christened in Holy Trinity Church. The inference that the marriage was forced upon the youth is natural but not inevitable; betrothal was legally binding at the time, and was sometimes regarded as conferring conjugal rights. Two additional children of the marriage, the twins Hamnet and Judith, were christened on February 2, 1585. Meanwhile the prosperity of the elder Shakespeares had declined, and William was impelled to seek a career outside Stratford.

The tradition that he spent some time as a country teacher is old but unverifiable. Because of the absence of records his early twenties are called the "lost years," and only one thing about them is certain — that at least some of these years were spent in winning a place in the acting profession. He may have begun as a provincial trouper, but by 1592 he was established in London and prominent enough to be attacked. In a pamphlet of that year, *Groatsworth of Wit*, the ailing Robert Greene complained of the neglect which university writers like himself had suffered from actors, one of whom was daring to set up as a playwright:

> . . . an upstart crow beautified with our feathers, that with his *Tiger's heart wrapt in a player's hide* supposes he is as well able to bombast out a blank verse as the best of you, and being an absolute Johannes-factotum, is in his own conceit the only Shake-scene in a country.

The pun on his name, and the parody of his line "O tiger's heart wrapt in a woman's hide" (*III Henry VI*), pointed clearly to Shakespeare. Some of his admirers protested, and Henry Chettle, the editor of Greene's pamphlet, saw fit to apologize:

> I am as sorry as if the original fault had been my fault, because myself have seen his demeanor no less civil than he excellent in the quality he professes. Besides divers of worship have reported his uprightness of dealing, which argues his honesty, and his facetious grace in writing that approves his art. (Prefatory epistle, *Kind Heart's Dream*)

The plague closed the London theatres for many months in 1593–94, denying the actors their livelihood. To this period belong Shakespeare's two narrative poems, *Venus and Adonis* and *Rape of Lucrece*, both dedicated to the Earl

8

of Southampton. No doubt the poet was rewarded with a gift of money as usual in such cases, but he did no further dedicating and we have no reliable information on whether Southampton, or anyone else, became his regular patron. His sonnets, first mentioned in 1598 and published without his consent in 1609, are intimate without being explicitly autobiographical. They seem to commemorate the poet's friendship with an idealized youth, rivalry with a more favored poet, and love affair with a dark mistress; and his bitterness when the mistress betrays him in conjunction with the friend; but it is difficult to decide precisely what the "story" is, impossible to decide whether it is fictional or true. The real distinction of the sonnets, at least of those not purely conventional, rests in the universality of the thoughts and moods they express, and in their poignancy and beauty.

In 1594 was formed the theatrical company known until 1603 as the Lord Chamberlain's Men, thereafter as the King's Men. Its original membership included, besides Shakespeare, the beloved clown Will Kempe and the famous actor Richard Burbage. The company acted in various London theatres and even toured the provinces, but it is chiefly associated in our minds with the Globe Theatre built on the south bank of the Thames in 1599. Shakespeare was an actor and joint owner of this company (and its Globe) through the remainder of his creative years. His plays, written at the average rate of two a year, together with Burbage's acting won it its place of leadership among the London companies.

Individual plays began to appear in print, in editions both honest and piratical, and the publishers became increasingly aware of the value of Shakespeare's name on the title pages. As early as 1598 he was hailed as the leading English dramatist in the *Palladis Tamia* of Francis Meres:

As Plautus and Seneca are accounted the best for Comedy and Tragedy among the Latins, so Shakespeare among the English is the most excellent in both kinds for the stage: for Comedy, witness his *Gentlemen of Verona*, his *Errors*, his *Love labors lost*, his *Love labors won [Taming of the Shrew?]*, his *Midsummers night dream*, & his *Merchant of Venice*; for Tragedy, his *Richard the 2*, *Richard the 3*, *Henry the 4*, *King John*, *Titus Andronicus*, and his *Romeo and Juliet*.

The note is valuable, both in indicating Shakespeare's prestige and in helping us to establish a chronology. In the second half of his writing career, history plays gave place to the great tragedies; and farces and light comedies gave place to the problem plays and symbolic romances. In 1623, seven years after his death, his former fellow actors, John Hemming and Henry Condell, cooperated with a group of London printers in bringing out his plays in collected form. The volume is generally known as the First Folio.

Shakespeare had never severed his relations with Stratford. His wife and children may sometimes have shared his London lodgings, but their home was Stratford. His son Hamnet was buried there in 1596, and his daughters Susanna and Judith were married there in 1607 and 1616 respectively. (His father, for whom he had secured a coat of arms and thus the privilege of writing himself gentleman, died in 1601, his mother in 1608.) His considerable earnings in London, as actor-sharer, part owner of the Globe, and playwright, were invested chiefly in Stratford property. In 1597 he purchased for £60 New Place, one of the two most imposing residences in the town. A number of other business transactions, as well as minor episodes in his career, have left documentary records. By 1611 he was in a position to retire, and he seems gradually to have withdrawn from theatrical activity in order to live in Stratford. In March, 1616, he made a will, leaving token bequests to Burbage, Hemming, and Condell, but the bulk of his estate to his family. The most famous feature of the will, the bequest of the second-best bed to his wife, reveals nothing about Shakespeare's marriage; the quaintness of the provision seems commonplace to those familiar with ancient testaments. Shakespeare died April 23, 1616, and was buried in the Stratford church where he had been christened. Within seven years a monument was erected to his memory on the north wall of the chancel. Its portrait bust and the Droeshout engraving on the title page of the First Folio provide the only likenesses with an established claim to authenticity. The best verbal vignette was written by his rival Ben Jonson, the more impressive for being imbedded in a context mainly critical:

> ... I loved the man, and do honor his memory (on this side idolatry) as much as any. He was indeed honest, and of an open and free nature: he had an excellent fancy, brave notions, and gentle expressions. . . . (*Timber or Discoveries,* c. 1623-30)

❈

The reader of Shakespeare's plays is aided by a general knowledge of the way in which they were staged. The King's Men acquired a roofed and artificially lighted theatre only toward the close of Shakespeare's career, and then only for winter use. Nearly all his plays were designed for performance in such structures as the Globe—a three-tiered amphitheatre with a large rectangular platform extending to the center of its yard. The plays were staged by daylight, by large casts brilliantly costumed, but with only a minimum of properties, without scenery, and quite possibly without intermissions. There was a rear stage balcony for action "above," and a curtained rear recess for "discoveries" and other special effects, but by far the major portion of any play was enacted upon the projecting platform, with episode following episode in swift succession, and with shifts of time and place signaled the audience only by the momentary clearing of the stage between the episodes. Information about the identity of the characters and, when necessary, about the time and place of the action was incorporated in the dialogue. No additional indications of place have been inserted in the present editions; these are apt to obscure the original fluidity of structure, with the emphasis upon action and speech rather than scenic background. The acting, including that of the youthful apprentices to the profession who performed the parts of women, was highly skillful, with a premium placed upon grace of gesture and beauty of diction. The audiences, a cross section of the general public, commonly numbered a thousand, sometimes more than two thousand. Judged by the type of plays they applauded, these audiences were not only large but also perceptive.

THE TEXTS OF THE PLAYS

About half of Shakespeare's plays appeared in print for the first time in the folio volume of 1623. The others had been published individually, usually in quarto volumes, during his lifetime or in the six years following his death. The copy used by the printers of the quartos varied greatly in merit, sometimes representing Shakespeare's true text, sometimes only a debased version of that text. The copy used by the printers of the folio also varied in merit, but was chosen with care. Since it consisted of the best available manuscripts, or the more acceptable quartos (although frequently in editions other than the first), or of quartos corrected by reference to manuscripts, we have good or reasonably good texts of most of the thirty-seven plays.

In the present series, the plays have been newly edited from quarto or folio texts depending, when a choice offered, upon which is now regarded by bibliographical specialists as the more authoritative. The ideal has been to reproduce the chosen texts with as few alterations as possible, beyond occasional relineation, expansion of abbreviations, and modernization of punctuation and spelling. Emendation is held to a minimum, and such material as has been added, in the way of stage directions and lines supplied by an alternative text, has been enclosed in square brackets.

None of the plays printed in Shakespeare's lifetime were divided into acts and scenes, and the inference is that the author's own manuscripts were not so divided. In the folio collection, some of the plays remained undivided, some were divided into acts, and some were divided into acts and scenes. During the eighteenth century all of the plays were divided into acts and scenes, and in the Cambridge edition of the mid-nineteenth century, from which the influential Globe text derived, this division was more or less regularized and the lines were numbered. Many useful works of reference employ the act-scene-line apparatus established by the Globe text.

Since the act-scene division thus established is obviously convenient, but is of very dubious authority so far as Shakespeare's own structural principles are concerned, or the original manner of staging his plays, a problem is presented to modern editors. In the present series the act-scene division of the Globe text is retained marginally, and may be viewed as a reference aid like the line numbering. A printer's ornament marks the points of division when these points have been determined by a cleared stage indicating a shift of time and place in the action of the play, or when no harm results from the editorial assumption that there is such a shift. However, at those points where the established division is clearly misleading — that is, where continuous action has been split up into separate "scenes" — the ornament is omitted and the distortion corrected. This mechanical expedient seemed the best means of combining utility and accuracy.

The General Editor.

INTRODUCTION

Romeo and Juliet is a play of young love. No other conveys so well the impetuous, idealistic passion of youth. The hero and heroine are not remarkable except in the overwhelming strength of their love for each other. Readers who love deeply may find here the idealized utterance of their feelings, and those who do not love deeply are led to wish that they could. The universal longing for a perfect romantic love, for the union of physical desire with selfless self-surrender, finds full expression in this play and makes it what Georg Brandes has called the great typical love-tragedy of the world.

That this appeal to a universal longing in human nature is the true secret of the play's success is witnessed by the great popularity of the balcony scene in Act II, which is not at all the dramatic climax of the play but is usually the scene most clearly remembered. In former centuries the Library of Oxford University kept its folio copy of Shakespeare's works chained to a desk at which students could stand and read. The well-thumbed pages of the balcony scene and of the parting scene in Act III give mute evidence that for young Oxonians these utterances of love were the most popular passages in all of Shakespeare's works.

Indeed, Shakespeare's finest achievement in this play is the successful portrayal of passionate physical love in terms of purity and innocence. The suggestive wink and the salacious leer are present in the jestings of the Nurse and the innuendoes of Mercutio, but these merely serve as contrasts to what Romeo and Juliet feel within themselves. When Juliet, soliloquizing, expresses her eager anticipation of her wedding night, she does not appear immodest but innocent in the best sense. Her passion for Romeo is ennobling, and the same is true of Romeo's love for her. The completeness of their devotion to each other leads them to ironic, untimely death; yet we cannot feel that this is wholly a defeat, for their love has risen superior to the storms of circumstance. In the words of Professor van Kranendonk, late of Amsterdam: "The poet has placed this springtime love in so intense a poetic light that an afterglow still remains over the somber ending. When we hear the names of Romeo and Juliet, we do not think first of all (as with Othello and Desdemona) about their pain, their misery, and their terrible undoing, but about their happiness together."

In style and manner, *Romeo and Juliet* seems nearer to *A Midsummer Night's Dream* than to Shakespeare's other plays. One finds the same intense lyricism, the same dependence upon rhymed couplets, the same enchantment of moonlight scenes, and the same interest in fairy lore. Finally, in *A Midsummer Night's Dream* there occurs a passage which seems to contain the theme enlarged upon in *Romeo and Juliet*. Lysander laments that in stories of the past "the course of true love never did run smooth" and that mutual happiness seldom endured, passing like a sound, a shadow, a dream, a flash of lightning swallowed up in darkness. "So quick bright things come to confusion," Lysander concludes, to which Hermia replies, "If then true lovers have been ever crossed,/It stands as an edict in destiny." These lines anticipate the "star-crossed lovers" of the Prologue to *Romeo and Juliet* and suggest that the evanescence of "bright things," particularly of young love, is a key to the mood in which the later play was written.

For some years scholars have debated the relative dates of these two plays. Internal evidence, while indicating 1594–95 as the date of *A Midsummer Night's Dream,* seemed to place *Romeo and Juliet* in 1591. In the Nurse's first scene, she says, "'Tis since the earthquake now eleven years," a line which has the earmarks of a topical allusion. If she refers to the much-publicized earthquake which shook England on April 6, 1580, then the play should be dated in 1591, a date which on other grounds seems much too early. Recent scholarship, however, has given us a choice of earthquakes, since one occurred in Dorsetshire in 1583 and one in Kent in 1585. A "terrible earthquake" which occurred on the Continent on March 1, 1584, is described in William Covell's *Polimanteia* (1595), a book which also praised "Sweet Shakspeare." It is therefore obvious that the earthquake could date *Romeo and Juliet* in 1594, 1595, or 1596, just as well as in 1591.

Other methods of establishing the date have been attempted. The play opens "a fortnight and odd days" before Lammas Tide (August 1st). Calculating the position of the moon as described in the play yields 1596 as the only year that will fit astronomically. The first edition of the play, the quarto of 1597, is described on the title page as having been acted by "Lord Hunsdon's servants." Shakespeare's company was known by this title only from July 1596 to March 1597. A scholar who has compared the type face of this edition with other books issued by its printer, John Danter, concludes that the quarto was printed in February or March of 1597. Since it was a reported edition and was presumably not authorized by Shakespeare, it probably represented an attempt to exploit the popularity of a new play. We may therefore with some confidence assign the composition of the play to the middle of 1596, in which case the earthquake recalled by the Nurse would be the one which occurred in Kent on August 4, 1585. The play followed *A Midsummer Night's Dream* by slightly more than a year.

Shakespeare's source for this play was *The Tragicall Historye of Romeus and Iuliet, written first in Italian by Bandell, and now in Englishe by Ar. Br.* (1562). This work by Arthur Broke, or Brooke, is a long narrative poem based on the prose of Bandello (1554) through an intermediate French version by Pierre Boaistuau (1559). Before Bandello, elements of the story were used by Luigi da Porto (1525) and Masuccio Salernitano (1476). Broke's poem apparently created in England a vogue for "tragical histories" translated from Bandello, Boccaccio, and other prose romancers. In the two decades following 1562, extensive collections of these were published in prose by William Painter, Geoffrey Fenton, and George Pettie, and in verse by James Sandford, George Turbervile, Robert Smyth, and Richard Tarleton. Painter's work included a prose translation of the Romeo-Juliet story, but Shakespeare seems not to have used it. Broke tells us in his preface that he had recently seen a play on the same subject acted on the stage (probably at the Inns of Court), but it seems unlikely that this play came to Shakespeare's attention thirty years later, since no further performances or printings of it are recorded. His obvious source, and probably his only one, was Broke's poem.

Shakespeare's dramatic genius may be studied in the changes which he has made from Broke's narrative. He

18

has shortened the duration of the action from nine months to less than a week. Thus the hasty march of events becomes a major cause of the tragedy; there is not time to settle problems which greater leisure would have simplified. He has expanded Mercutio's role from a mere reference in Broke and has invented the two duels involving Tybalt, thereby enhancing Romeo's dilemma of love against honor; for in Broke's poem Romeo kills Tybalt accidentally while defending himself in a street brawl. He has taken from Broke almost every incident involving the Nurse, yet he has created in her affectionate, vulgar, easygoing personality one of his most original characters. Finally, he has portrayed in the Capulet household a remarkable study in family psychology.

In Bandello's story Juliet is eighteen years old, in Broke's poem she is sixteen, and in Shakespeare's play she is nearing her fourteenth birthday. Since Renaissance physiologists generally considered fourteen to mark the beginning of puberty (cf. *The Winter's Tale*, II, i, 147), Shakespeare apparently intended to picture Juliet's love for Romeo as first love, strengthened by the fact that she is just becoming emotionally aware of the meaning of love itself. (A similar purpose is evident in *The Tempest*, where Miranda is approximately the same age as Juliet.) In her emotions Juliet has suddenly become a woman, while in other respects she is still a child. Neither she nor her parents can quite understand this change; they consider her refusal to marry Paris childish willfulness, and she is too much in awe of them to tell them the truth.

Capulet is an old man married to a young woman. In spite of Lady Capulet's reference to her "old age," she is twenty-eight, only twice the age of her daughter. Capulet, however, had last attended a masquerade more than thirty years before and is now probably in his sixties. Since the earth had "swallowèd all my hopes" but Juliet, and since she is the only child born to Lady Capulet, Capulet must have had children by a former marriage. Lady Capulet has retained something of the awe of the child-bride for her older husband and defers to his judgment — and to his temper — in hastening the marriage with Paris. Her habit of deference to his wishes may have caused her to withhold from Juliet sympathy which she normally would have given. Capulet assumes the management of the household duties and dearly loves to plan big parties. Even among his laments for Juliet's death is a regret that it should "murder our solemnity," i.e., spoil the feast which he had planned. His domestic ménage is hardly that of a great Italian nobleman and perhaps more nearly resembles that of a wealthy burgher of Stratford, recalled from Shakespeare's youth.

The play also represents an advance in Shakespeare's ability to reproduce the language of young gentlemen. The badinage of Mercutio, Romeo, and Benvolio is a decided improvement over similar conversations in earlier plays. Mercutio's unique blend of critical acumen, delicate fancy, and obscene levity makes him a remarkable character creation. One critic suggests that Shakespeare was forced to kill Mercutio lest he "steal the show" from the major figures of the plot. Like Jaques and Falstaff in later plays, he exists more as a character portrayed for its own innate interest than as an essential participant in the dramatic action.

Unlike Shakespeare's later tragedies, *Romeo and Juliet* is a play of externals, of characters portrayed in their relationships with each other. Their motives and feelings are readily understandable. There is a minimum of introspective brooding, enigmatic utterance, and puzzlement over moral problems; instead, all is quick decision and rapid action. In later tragedies Shakespeare undertook to explore the secret recesses of the soul, but here he shows people in conflict with external circumstance. Their errors of judgment are not errors involving a consciousness of sin but are attributable to impetuous haste and unkind fate. Nothing is withheld from the reader; characters and their motives are revealed as completely as possible. The same lack of reticence is evident in the literary style, which abounds in conceits, plays on words, and luxuriant poetic descriptions. Perhaps it is the quality of complete representation of emotions and moods that has made the play a favorite with musical composers: Gounod, Berlioz, Tschaikowsky, Prokofiev, and Milhaud, among others.

In *Romeo and Juliet* Shakespeare exploits dramatic irony in abrupt reversals of situation. Romeo, despondent, goes unwillingly to Capulet's ball and is quickly raised to joy by his encounter with Juliet, only to find that she is his hereditary enemy. This obstacle overcome, his joy reaches a height with his wedding, but within a half hour he is plunged into despair after his duel with Tybalt. At the beginning of Act V, Romeo is cheerful because of a dream which seems to foretell his reunion with Juliet, but his hopes are quickly dashed by Balthasar's news of her death. The supreme instance of irony comes as he stands beside her in the sepulchre, observing that she looks as though alive, and then drinks the poison to join her in death. The audience knows that she really is alive and will awake in a few minutes. In David Garrick's acting version of the play (as in Bandello's story) Juliet awakes before Romeo dies, and he thus realizes the bitter irony of his situation. The questionable dramatic propriety of this ending has caused considerable debate among students of the play.

Shakespeare makes one other effective use of irony. When Capulet and his wife are scolding Juliet for her refusal to marry Paris, each petulantly expresses a wish for her death. "I would the fool were married to her grave," says Lady Capulet. Capulet says that they have only one child, "but now I see this one is one too much." They do not intend these statements seriously, as Juliet doubtless realizes, but their words are ominous of what is to come. They get what they ask for.

In recent years numerous attempts have been made to state a central theme for the play. One critic views it as a tragedy of unawareness. Capulet and Montague are unaware of the fateful issues which may hang upon their quarrel. Romeo and Juliet fall in love while unaware that they are hereditary enemies. Mercutio and Tybalt are both unaware of the true state of affairs when they fight their duel. In the chain of events leading to the final tragedy, even the servants play a part and are unaware of the results of their actions. The final scene, with Friar Laurence's long explanation, is dramatically justified because it brings Montague, Capulet, Lady Capulet, and the Prince to at least a partial awareness of their responsibility for what has happened. Supplementing this view of the play is one which finds it to be a study of the wholeness and complexity of things in human affairs. The issues of the feud may appear to be simple and clear, but in reality they are highly complex, giving rise to results which are completely unforeseen. The goodness or badness of human actions is relative, not absolute, an idea symbolically set forth in Friar Laurence's opening speech on herbs which are medicinal or poisonous according to the manner of their use.

Other clues to the meaning of the play may be found in the repetitive imagery employed by Shakespeare. The images of haste, of events rushing to a conclusion, are found throughout. When Romeo says, "I stand on sudden haste," Friar Laurence answers, "They stumble that run fast," and thus expresses one moral to be drawn from the play. Romeo and Mercutio symbolize their wit-combat by the wild-goose chase, a reckless cross-country horse race. "Swits and spurs," cries Romeo, using the imagery of speed. Numerous other instances may be found.

Closely allied to the imagery of haste is the violence expressed in the gunpowder image. The Friar warns that too impetuous love is like fire and powder, "which, as they kiss, consume." Romeo desires a poison that will expel life from his body like powder fired from a cannon. This may identify the Apothecary's poison as aconite, since elsewhere Shakespeare compares the action of aconite with that of "rash gunpowder" (2 *Henry IV*, IV, iv, 48). Violence is also expressed in the image of shipwreck which may end the voyage of life. Capulet compares Juliet weeping to a bark in danger from tempests. Romeo describes his death as the shipwreck of his "seasick weary bark." Earlier, after expressing a premonition that attendance at Capulet's party will cause his death, he resigns himself to Him "that hath the steerage of my course," anticipating his later images of the ship and the voyage of life.

Also repeated in the play is the image of Death as the lover of Juliet. She herself uses it, her father uses it beside her bier, and Romeo uses it most effectively in the final scene. The effect of this repeated image is to suggest that Juliet is foredoomed to die, that Death, personified, has claimed her for his own. It thus strengthens the ominous note of fate which is felt throughout the play.

23

INTRODUCTION

That *Romeo and Juliet* is a tragedy of fate can hardly be
doubted. Shakespeare says as much in the Prologue. The
lovers are marked for death; their fortunes are "crossed"
by the stars. The reason for their doom is likewise given:
only the shock of their deaths can force their parents to
end the senseless feud. At the end of the play Capulet calls
the lovers "poor sacrifices of our enmity," and the Prince
describes their deaths as Heaven's punishment of their
parents' hate. Romeo's premonition of death before going
to the party attributes it to "some consequence yet hanging
in the stars." The note of fate is struck repeatedly during
the play. "A greater power than we can contradict / Hath
thwarted our intents," says Friar Laurence to Juliet in the
tomb. The numerous mischances experienced by the lovers
are not fortuitous bad luck but represent the working out
of some hidden design. Critics who attack the play for
lacking inevitability have misunderstood Shakespeare's
dramatic technique. Like Hamlet's adventure with the
pirates, the sequence of mishaps here is deliberately made
so improbable that chance alone cannot explain it. Only
fate, or the will of Heaven, affords a sufficient explanation.

One finds it difficult to interpret this tragedy in Aris-
totelian terms, since the parents are really the ones who
have the "tragic flaw" and suffer the results of their folly,
as Lear does, in the deaths of their children. Yet the children,
not the parents, are the major figures of the play. Some
critics have named impetuosity as Romeo's "tragic flaw,"
but Romeo is less impetuous than Tybalt or Mercutio, and
one can hardly name as a "flaw" a quality which is pictured
as common to youth. It it true that greater placidity of
temperament and more deliberate speed might have averted
the tragedy under the given circumstances, yet the pattern

of circumstances might easily have been different and the will of fate have been accomplished just the same.

Shakespeare makes it clear that society is partly responsible for the tragedy. The feud between noble families was a matter of social convention. So was the necessity to take personal revenge for an insult to one's honor. Here there seems to be a topical allusion. Prince Escalus represents the view of Queen Elizabeth, whose government decreed that homicide in a duel should be punishable as murder. She was determined to stamp out duelling. Furthermore, the evil arising from any form of civil strife is a constantly reiterated theme in Elizabethan literature. Current social attitudes may be noted both in the Prince's edict against street fighting and in the cavalier disregard of it.

As might be expected, *Romeo and Juliet* has been a popular stage play, never more so than now, when each year sees from ten to twenty new productions by professional and amateur groups. What Hamlet is for the actor, Juliet is for the actress, a role which offers the fullest scope for the display of female histrionics. In past centuries Mrs. Betterton and Fanny Kemble made great successes in the part. In the present century Julia Marlowe, Eva Le Gallienne, Jane Cowl, and Katherine Cornell are among those who have played Juliet. The producer of this play always has a problem, for very few great actresses achieve eminence by the age of fourteen, and most of them are recognizably mature women trying to look young. To a lesser extent the same problem exists in casting the masculine roles. The producer must choose between the verisimilitude of a youthful cast and the more sophisticated acting of experienced players. Nevertheless, despite all difficulties, *Romeo and Juliet* is still constantly staged with success, and most of us can recall productions in which it proved as vivid and moving in the theatre as it always proves on the printed page.

University of Maine   JOHN E. HANKINS

Note on the text: An abridged and inaccurate version of *Romeo and Juliet*, evidently "reporting" the play in performance, was published in quarto in 1597. In 1599 appeared a good quarto, probably printed from Shakespeare's draft with some reference to the earlier quarto. A third quarto was printed from the second in 1609, and this was used as copy for the fourth quarto, undated, and the text of the first folio, 1623. The present edition follows the quarto of 1599, with faulty readings corrected with caution by reference to the quarto of 1597, and with few emendations. (All material departures from the text of the 1599 quarto are listed in an appendix, with the exception of added stage directions and adjusted cancellations; the two latter classes of departure are noted as they occur.) None of the early texts, including that of the folio, are divided into acts and scenes. The division supplied marginally in the present edition is that of the Globe text and is for purposes of reference only.

The Tragedy of
Romeo and Juliet

THE TRAGEDY OF
ROMEO AND JULIET

[Enter] Chorus.

Chorus. Two households, both alike in dignity,
    In fair Verona, where we lay our scene,
From ancient grudge break to new mutiny,
    Where civil blood makes civil hands unclean.
From forth the fatal loins of these two foes   5
    A pair of star-crossed lovers take their life;
Whose misadventured piteous overthrows
    Doth with their death bury their parents' strife.
The fearful passage of their death-marked love,
    And the continuance of their parents' rage,   10
Which, but their children's end, naught could remove,
    Is now the two hours' traffic of our stage;
The which if you with patient ears attend,
    What here shall miss, our toil shall strive to mend. *[Exit.]*

Pro., 3 *mutiny* outbursts of violence   4 *civil . . . civil* citizens' . . . fellow citizens'   6 *star-crossed* thwarted by adverse stars   9 *death-marked* foredoomed to death   12 *two . . . stage* our stage-business for the next two hours

I, i   *Enter Sampson and Gregory, with swords and bucklers, of
the house of Capulet.*

Sampson. Gregory, on my word, we'll not carry coals.

Gregory. No, for then we should be colliers.

Sampson. I mean, an we be in choler, we'll draw.

Gregory. Ay, while you live, draw your neck out of collar.

5 *Sampson.* I strike quickly, being moved.

Gregory. But thou art not quickly moved to strike.

Sampson. A dog of the house of Montague moves me.

Gregory. To move is to stir, and to be valiant is to stand.
Therefore, if thou art moved, thou runn'st away.

10 *Sampson.* A dog of that house shall move me to stand. I
will take the wall of any man or maid of Montague's.

Gregory. That shows thee a weak slave; for the weakest
goes to the wall.

Sampson. 'Tis true; and therefore women, being the weaker
15   vessels, are ever thrust to the wall. Therefore I will push
Montague's men from the wall and thrust his maids to
the wall.

Gregory. The quarrel is between our masters, and us their
men.

20 *Sampson.* 'Tis all one. I will show myself a tyrant. When I
have fought with the men, I will be cruel with the maids
— I will cut off their heads.

Gregory. The heads of the maids?

Sampson. Ay, the heads of the maids, or their maidenheads.
25   Take it in what sense thou wilt.

Gregory. They must take it in sense that feel it.

I, i, 1 *carry coals* i.e. suffer insults   2 *colliers* coal dealers   3 *an* if   *choler*
anger   *draw* draw our swords   4 *collar* hangman's noose   11 *take the wall*
pass on the inner and cleaner part of the sidewalk   12–13 *the weakest . . .
wall* i.e. is pushed from his place (proverbial)   14–15 *weaker vessels* (cf. 1
Peter 3:7)   25–26 *sense . . . sense* meaning . . . physical sensation

Sampson. Me they shall feel while I am able to stand; and
   'tis known I am a pretty piece of flesh.
Gregory. 'Tis well thou art not fish; if thou hadst, thou
   hadst been poor-John. Draw thy tool! Here comes two of 30
   the house of Montagues.

Enter two other Servingmen [Abram and Balthasar].

Sampson. My naked weapon is out. Quarrel! I will back
   thee.
Gregory. How? turn thy back and run?
Sampson. Fear me not.   35
Gregory. No, marry. I fear thee!
Sampson. Let us take the law of our sides; let them begin.
Gregory. I will frown as I pass by, and let them take it as
   they list.
Sampson. Nay, as they dare. I will bite my thumb at them, 40
   which is disgrace to them if they bear it.
Abram. Do you bite your thumb at us, sir?
Sampson. I do bite my thumb, sir.
Abram. Do you bite your thumb at us, sir?
Sampson. [aside to Gregory] Is the law of our side if I say ay? 45
Gregory. [aside to Sampson] No.
Sampson. No, sir, I do not bite my thumb at you, sir; but
   I bite my thumb, sir.
Gregory. Do you quarrel, sir?
Abram. Quarrel, sir? No, sir.   50
Sampson. But if you do, sir, I am for you. I serve as good
   a man as you.

28, 29 *flesh, fish* (alluding to the proverb 'Neither fish nor flesh')   30 *poor-
John* dried hake, the cheapest fish   *tool* sword (with ribald innuendo)
36 *marry* indeed (originally an oath by the Virgin Mary)   *I fear thee* to
suppose me afraid of you is ridiculous   37 *take . . . of* have the law on
40 *bite my thumb* (an insulting gesture)

31

Abram. No better.
Sampson. Well, sir.

Enter Benvolio.

55 *Gregory.* [*aside to Sampson*] Say 'better.' Here comes one of
   my master's kinsmen.
Sampson. Yes, better, sir.
Abram. You lie.
Sampson. Draw, if you be men. Gregory, remember thy
60   swashing blow.   *They fight.*
Benvolio. Part, fools!
   Put up your swords. You know not what you do.

Enter Tybalt.

Tybalt. What, art thou drawn among these heartless hinds?
   Turn thee, Benvolio! look upon thy death.
65 *Benvolio.* I do but keep the peace. Put up thy sword,
   Or manage it to part these men with me.
Tybalt. What, drawn, and talk of peace? I hate the word
   As I hate hell, all Montagues, and thee.
   Have at thee, coward!   *[They fight.]*

*Enter [an Officer, and] three or four Citizens with clubs
   or partisans.*

70 *Officer.* Clubs, bills, and partisans! Strike! beat them down!
Citizens. Down with the Capulets! Down with the Montagues!

Enter old Capulet in his gown, and his Wife.

Capulet. What noise is this? Give me my long sword, ho!
Wife. A crutch, a crutch! Why call you for a sword?

60 *swashing* smashing   63 *heartless hinds* cowardly servants   70 *bills,
partisans* long-shafted weapons with combined spear-head and cutting-
blade

Capulet. My sword, I say! Old Montague is come   75
  And flourishes his blade in spite of me.

      Enter old Montague and his Wife.

Montague. Thou villain Capulet! — Hold me not, let me go.
Montague's Wife. Thou shalt not stir one foot to seek a foe.

      Enter Prince Escalus, with his Train.

Prince. Rebellious subjects, enemies to peace,
  Profaners of this neighbor-stainèd steel —   80
  Will they not hear? What, ho! you men, you beasts,
  That quench the fire of your pernicious rage
  With purple fountains issuing from your veins!
  On pain of torture, from those bloody hands
  Throw your mistemperèd weapons to the ground   85
  And hear the sentence of your movèd prince.
  Three civil brawls, bred of an airy word
  By thee, old Capulet, and Montague,
  Have thrice disturbed the quiet of our streets
  And made Verona's ancient citizens   90
  Cast by their grave beseeming ornaments
  To wield old partisans, in hands as old,
  Cank'red with peace, to part your cank'red hate.
  If ever you disturb our streets again,
  Your lives shall pay the forfeit of the peace.   95
  For this time all the rest depart away.
  You, Capulet, shall go along with me;
  And, Montague, come you this afternoon,
  To know our farther pleasure in this case,

---

76 *in spite of* in defiance of 85 *mistemperèd* (1) badly made (2) used for
a bad purpose 87 *airy* made with breath 90 *ancient citizens* a volunteer
guard of older men 91 *grave beseeming ornaments* staffs and costumes
appropriate for the aged 93 *Cank'red . . . cank'red* rusted . . . malignant

100   To old Freetown, our common judgment place.
       Once more, on pain of death, all men depart.
                    Exeunt [all but Montague, his Wife, and Benvolio].
       Montague. Who set this ancient quarrel new abroach?
       Speak, nephew, were you by when it began?
       Benvolio. Here were the servants of your adversary
105   And yours, close fighting ere I did approach.
       I drew to part them. In the instant came
       The fiery Tybalt, with his sword prepared;
       Which, as he breathed defiance to my ears,
       He swung about his head and cut the winds,
110   Who, nothing hurt withal, hissed him in scorn.
       While we were interchanging thrusts and blows,
       Came more and more, and fought on part and part,
       Till the Prince came, who parted either part.
       Montague's Wife. O, where is Romeo? Saw you him
                    to-day?
115   Right glad I am he was not at this fray.
       Benvolio. Madam, an hour before the worshipped sun
       Peered forth the golden window of the East,
       A troubled mind drave me to walk abroad;
       Where, underneath the grove of sycamore
120   That westward rooteth from this city side,
       So early walking did I see your son.
       Towards him I made, but he was ware of me
       And stole into the covert of the wood.
       I, measuring his affections by my own,
125   Which then most sought where most might not be found,
       Being one too many by my weary self,

100 *Freetown* (Broke's translation of *Villafranca*)   102 *set . . . abroach*
reopened this quarrel of long standing   110 *Who* which   *nothing* not at
all   *withal* therewith   122 *ware* aware, wary   124 *affections* inclinations,
feelings   125 *most sought . . . found* i.e. desired solitude

34

Pursued my humor, not pursuing his,
And gladly shunned who gladly fled from me.
Montague. Many a morning hath he there been seen,
    With tears augmenting the fresh morning's dew,   130
    Adding to clouds more clouds with his deep sighs;
    But all so soon as the all-cheering sun
    Should in the farthest East begin to draw
    The shady curtains from Aurora's bed,
    Away from light steals home my heavy son   135
    And private in his chamber pens himself,
    Shuts up his windows, locks fair daylight out,
    And makes himself an artificial night.
    Black and portentous must this humor prove
    Unless good counsel may the cause remove.   140
Benvolio. My noble uncle, do you know the cause?
Montague. I neither know it nor can learn of him.
Benvolio. Have you importuned him by any means?
Montague. Both by myself and many other friends;
    But he, his own affections' counsellor,   145
    Is to himself — I will not say how true —
    But to himself so secret and so close,
    So far from sounding and discovery,
    As is the bud bit with an envious worm
    Ere he can spread his sweet leaves to the air   150
    Or dedicate his beauty to the sun.
    Could we but learn from whence his sorrows grow,
    We would as willingly give cure as know.

Enter Romeo.

Benvolio. See, where he comes. So please you step aside,
    I'll know his grievance, or be much denied.   155

134 *Aurora* the dawn   135 *heavy* melancholy   139 *humor* mood   148
sounding being measured (as water-depth is measured with a plummet line)

Montague. I would thou wert so happy by thy stay
  To hear true shrift. Come, madam, let's away.
                              Exeunt [Montague and Wife].
Benvolio. Good morrow, cousin.
Romeo.   Is the day so young?
Benvolio. But new struck nine.
Romeo.   Ay me! sad hours seem long.
160 Was that my father that went hence so fast?
Benvolio. It was. What sadness lengthens Romeo's hours?
Romeo. Not having that which having makes them short.
Benvolio. In love?
Romeo. Out —
165 *Benvolio.* Of love?
Romeo. Out of her favor where I am in love.
Benvolio. Alas that love, so gentle in his view,
  Should be so tyrannous and rough in proof!
Romeo. Alas that love, whose view is muffled still,
170 Should without eyes see pathways to his will!
  Where shall we dine? O me! What fray was here?
  Yet tell me not, for I have heard it all.
  Here's much to do with hate, but more with love.
  Why then, O brawling love, O loving hate,
175 O anything, of nothing first create!
  O heavy lightness, serious vanity,
  Misshapen chaos of well-seeming forms,
  Feather of lead, bright smoke, cold fire, sick health,
  Still-waking sleep, that is not what it is!
180 This love feel I, that feel no love in this.
  Dost thou not laugh?

---

157 *shrift* confession 158 *morrow* morning 167 *view* appearance 168 *in proof* in being experienced 169 *view* sight *muffled* blindfolded 173–80 *Here's . . . this* (the rhetorical name for such paradoxes is oxymoron; cf. III, ii, 73–85)

Benvolio.   No, coz, I rather weep.
Romeo. Good heart, at what?
Benvolio.   At thy good heart's oppression.
Romeo. Why, such is love's transgression.
　　Griefs of mine own lie heavy in my breast,
　　Which thou wilt propagate, to have it prest   185
　　With more of thine. This love that thou hast shown
　　Doth add more grief to too much of mine own.
　　Love is a smoke raised with the fume of sighs;
　　Being purged, a fire sparkling in lovers' eyes;
　　Being vexed, a sea nourished with lovers' tears.   190
　　What is it else? A madness most discreet,
　　A choking gall, and a preserving sweet.
　　Farewell, my coz.
Benvolio.   Soft! I will go along.
　　An if you leave me so, you do me wrong.
Romeo. Tut! I have lost myself; I am not here;   195
　　This is not Romeo, he's some other where.
Benvolio. Tell me in sadness, who is that you love?
Romeo. What, shall I groan and tell thee?
Benvolio.   Groan? Why, no;
　　But sadly tell me who.
Romeo. Bid a sick man in sadness make his will.   200
　　Ah, word ill urged to one that is so ill!
　　In sadness, cousin, I do love a woman.
Benvolio. I aimed so near when I supposed you loved.
Romeo. A right good markman. And she's fair I love.
Benvolio. A right fair mark, fair coz, is soonest hit.   205
Romeo. Well, in that hit you miss. She'll not be hit

181 *coz* cousin 184–87 *Griefs . . . own* your sorrow for my grief grieves
me further to have caused you sorrow 195 *lost* (so both Q2 and Q1, but
the emendation 'left' has been cogently suggested) 197 *in sadness* seriously
205 *fair mark* bright clean target

37

With Cupid's arrow. She hath Dian's wit,
And, in strong proof of chastity well armed,
From Love's weak childish bow she lives unharmed.
210 She will not stay the siege of loving terms,
Nor bide th' encounter of assailing eyes,
Nor ope her lap to saint-seducing gold.
O, she is rich in beauty; only poor
That, when she dies, with beauty dies her store.
215 *Benvolio.* Then she hath sworn that she will still live chaste?
Romeo. She hath, and in that sparing makes huge waste;
For beauty, starved with her severity,
Cuts beauty off from all posterity.
She is too fair, too wise, wisely too fair,
220 To merit bliss by making me despair.
She hath forsworn to love, and in that vow
Do I live dead that live to tell it now.
Benvolio. Be ruled by me; forget to think of her.
Romeo. O, teach me how I should forget to think!
225 *Benvolio.* By giving liberty unto thine eyes.
Examine other beauties.
Romeo.   'Tis the way
To call hers (exquisite) in question more.
These happy masks that kiss fair ladies' brows,
Being black puts us in mind they hide the fair.
230 He that is strucken blind cannot forget
The precious treasure of his eyesight lost.
Show me a mistress that is passing fair,
What doth her beauty serve but as a note

207 *Dian* Diana, virgin goddess and huntress 208 *proof* armor 209 *un-harmed* (from Q1; Q2 reads 'uncharmed,' perhaps correctly) 210–11 *She . . . eyes* i.e. she gives me no chance to woo her 214 *with . . . store* she will leave no children to perpetuate her beauty 215 *still* always 216 *sparing* miserly economy 220 *bliss* heaven 227 *in question* to my mind 232 *passing* surpassingly

Where I may read who passed that passing fair?
Farewell. Thou canst not teach me to forget.   235
Benvolio. I'll pay that doctrine, or else die in debt. *Exeunt.*

❧

Enter Capulet, County Paris, and the Clown [a Servant].   I, ii

Capulet. But Montague is bound as well as I,
   In penalty alike; and 'tis not hard, I think,
   For men so old as we to keep the peace.
Paris. Of honorable reckoning are you both,
   And pity 'tis you lived at odds so long.   5
   But now, my lord, what say you to my suit?
Capulet. But saying o'er what I have said before:
   My child is yet a stranger in the world,
   She hath not seen the change of fourteen years;
   Let two more summers wither in their pride   10
   Ere we may think her ripe to be a bride.
Paris. Younger than she are happy mothers made.
Capulet. And too soon marred are those so early made.
   The earth hath swallowèd all my hopes but she;
   She is the hopeful lady of my earth.   15
   But woo her, gentle Paris, get her heart;
   My will to her consent is but a part.
   An she agree, within her scope of choice
   Lies my consent and fair according voice.
   This night I hold an old accustomed feast,   20

236 *pay that doctrine* convince you otherwise I, ii, 1 *bound* under bond
4 *reckoning* reputation 8 *world* world of society 13 *marred* disfigured by
childbirth 14 *hopes* children 18 *scope* range 19 *according* harmoniously
agreeing 20 *old accustomed* by custom of long standing

Whereto I have invited many a guest,
Such as I love; and you among the store,
One more, most welcome, makes my number more.
At my poor house look to behold this night
25   Earth-treading stars that make dark heaven light.
Such comfort as do lusty young men feel
When well-apparelled April on the heel
Of limping Winter treads, even such delight
Among fresh fennel buds shall you this night
30   Inherit at my house. Hear all, all see,
And like her most whose merit most shall be;
Which, on more view of many, mine, being one,
May stand in number, though in reck'ning none.
Come, go with me. *[to Servant, giving him a paper]* Go,
     sirrah, trudge about
35   Through fair Verona; find those persons out
Whose names are written there, and to them say,
My house and welcome on their pleasure stay.
                              Exit [with Paris].
Servant. Find them out whose names are written here? It
is written that the shoemaker should meddle with his
40   yard and the tailor with his last, the fisher with his pencil
and the painter with his nets; but I am sent to find those
persons whose names are here writ, and can never find
what names the writing person hath here writ. I must
to the learned. In good time!

25 *stars* i.e. maidens   27 *April* (Venus' month, the season of lovemaking)
29 *fennel* a flowering herb associated with stimulation and enticement
32-33 *Which . . . none* my daughter will be numerically counted among
those present, but possibly not among those you would wish to marry
after seeing them all (cf. the common saying 'One is no number')   34
sirrah (a familiar form of address, used with servants and sometimes with
friends)   40-41 *yard, last, pencil, nets* (occupational tools humorously
reversed)   42 *find* find out (since I cannot read)   44 *In good time* help
comes just when I need it

Enter Benvolio and Romeo.

Benvolio. Tut, man, one fire burns out another's burning; 45
 One pain is less'ned by another's anguish;
 Turn giddy, and be holp by backward turning;
 One desperate grief cures with another's languish.
 Take thou some new infection to thy eye,
 And the rank poison of the old will die. 50
Romeo. Your plantain leaf is excellent for that.
Benvolio. For what, I pray thee?
Romeo.   For your broken shin.
Benvolio. Why, Romeo, art thou mad?
Romeo. Not mad, but bound more than a madman is;
 Shut up in prison, kept without my food, 55
 Whipped and tormented and — God-den, good fellow.
Servant. God gi' go-den. I pray, sir, can you read?
Romeo. Ay, mine own fortune in my misery.
Servant. Perhaps you have learned it without book. But I
 pray, can you read anything you see? 60
Romeo. Ay, if I know the letters and the language.
Servant. Ye say honestly. Rest you merry.
Romeo. Stay, fellow; I can read.   *He reads the letter.*
 'Signior Martino and his wife and daughters;
 County Anselmo and his beauteous sisters; 65
 The lady widow of Vitruvio;
 Signior Placentio and his lovely nieces;
 Mercutio and his brother Valentine;

---

45 *one . . . burning* (proverb used often by Shakespeare) 46 *another's
anguish* anguish from another pain 47 *Turn . . . turning* when giddy from
whirling around, be helped by reversing direction 49 *infection* (figuratively used, but taken literally by Romeo) 54–56 *bound . . . tormented*
(customary treatment of madmen) 56 *God-den* good evening (used after
12:00 noon; cf. II, iv, 105) 61 *if I know* (the servant takes this to mean
'only if I have memorized the appearance of')

41

Mine uncle Capulet, his wife, and daughters;
70 My fair niece Rosaline and Livia;
Signior Valentio and his cousin Tybalt;
Lucio and the lively Helena.'
A fair assembly. Whither should they come?
Servant. Up.
75 *Romeo.* Whither? To supper?
Servant. To our house.
Romeo. Whose house?
Servant. My master's.
Romeo. Indeed I should have asked you that before.
80 *Servant.* Now I'll tell you without asking. My master is
the great rich Capulet; and if you be not of the house of
Montagues, I pray come and crush a cup of wine. Rest
you merry.   *[Exit.]*
Benvolio. At this same ancient feast of Capulet's
85 Sups the fair Rosaline whom thou so loves;
With all the admirèd beauties of Verona.
Go thither, and with unattainted eye
Compare her face with some that I shall show,
And I will make thee think thy swan a crow.
90 *Romeo.* When the devout religion of mine eye
Maintains such falsehood, then turn tears to fires;
And these, who, often drowned, could never die,
Transparent heretics, be burnt for liars!
One fairer than my love? The all-seeing sun
95 Ne'er saw her match since first the world begun.
Benvolio. Tut! you saw her fair, none else being by,
Herself poised with herself in either eye;
But in that crystal scales let there be weighed

82 *crush* drink   87 *unattainted* unprejudiced   92 *these* these eyes   *drowned*
i.e. in tears   98 *crystal scales* (Romeo's two eyes are compared to the two
ends of a pair of balances)

Your lady's love against some other maid
That I will show you shining at this feast,   100
And she shall scant show well that now seems best.
Romeo. I'll go along, no such sight to be shown,
   But to rejoice in splendor of my own.   *[Exeunt.]*

❁

Enter Capulet's Wife, and Nurse.   I, iii

Wife. Nurse, where's my daughter? Call her forth to me.
Nurse. Now, by my maidenhead at twelve year old,
   I bade her come. What, lamb! what, ladybird!
   God forbid, where's this girl? What, Juliet!

Enter Juliet.

Juliet. How now? Who calls?
Nurse.   Your mother.
Juliet.   Madam, I am here.   5
   What is your will?
Wife. This is the matter — Nurse, give leave awhile,
   We must talk in secret. Nurse, come back again;
   I have rememb'red me, thou 's hear our counsel.
   Thou knowest my daughter's of a pretty age.   10
Nurse. Faith, I can tell her age unto an hour.
Wife. She's not fourteen.
Nurse.   I'll lay fourteen of my teeth —
   And yet, to my teen be it spoken, I have but four —
   She's not fourteen. How long is it now
   To Lammastide?
Wife.   A fortnight and odd days.   15

101 *scant* scarcely   I, iii, 7 *give leave* leave us   9 *thou 's* thou shalt   13 *teen*
sorrow   15 *Lammastide* August 1st

Nurse. Even or odd, of all days in the year,
  Come Lammas Eve at night shall she be fourteen.
  Susan and she (God rest all Christian souls!)
  Were of an age. Well, Susan is with God;
20 She was too good for me. But, as I said,
  On Lammas Eve at night shall she be fourteen;
  That shall she, marry; I remember it well.
  'Tis since the earthquake now eleven years;
  And she was weaned (I never shall forget it),
25 Of all the days of the year, upon that day;
  For I had then laid wormwood to my dug,
  Sitting in the sun under the dovehouse wall.
  My lord and you were then at Mantua.
  Nay, I do bear a brain. But, as I said,
30 When it did taste the wormwood on the nipple
  Of my dug and felt it bitter, pretty fool,
  To see it tetchy and fall out with the dug!
  Shake, quoth the dovehouse! 'Twas no need, I trow,
  To bid me trudge.
35 And since that time it is eleven years,
  For then she could stand high-lone; nay, by th' rood,
  She could have run and waddled all about;
  For even the day before, she broke her brow;
  And then my husband (God be with his soul!
40 'A was a merry man) took up the child.
  'Yea,' quoth he, 'dost thou fall upon thy face?
  Thou wilt fall backward when thou hast more wit;
  Wilt thou not, Jule?' and, by my holidam,

23 *earthquake* (see Introduction, page 17)   29 *bear a brain* keep my mental
powers   32 *tetchy* fretful   33 *Shake . . . dovehouse* i.e. the dovehouse creaked
from the earthquake   *trow* believe   34 *trudge* run away   36 *high-lone* alone
rood cross   43 *holidam* halidom, holy relic

The pretty wretch left crying and said 'Ay.'
To see now how a jest shall come about!   45
I warrant, an I should live a thousand years,
I never should forget it. 'Wilt thou not, Jule?' quoth he,
And, pretty fool, it stinted and said 'Ay.'
Wife. Enough of this. I pray thee hold thy peace.
Nurse. Yes, madam. Yet I cannot choose but laugh   50
  To think it should leave crying and say 'Ay.'
  And yet, I warrant, it had upon it brow
  A bump as big as a young cock'rel's stone;
  A perilous knock; and it cried bitterly.
  'Yea,' quoth my husband, 'fall'st upon thy face?   55
  Thou wilt fall backward when thou comest to age;
  Wilt thou not, Jule?' It stinted and said 'Ay.'
Juliet. And stint thou too, I pray thee, nurse, say I.
Nurse. Peace, I have done. God mark thee to his grace!
  Thou wast the prettiest babe that e'er I nursed.   60
  An I might live to see thee married once,
  I have my wish.
Wife. Marry, that 'marry' is the very theme
  I came to talk of. Tell me, daughter Juliet,
  How stands your disposition to be married?   65
Juliet. It is an honor that I dream not of.
Nurse. An honor? Were not I thine only nurse,
  I would say thou hadst sucked wisdom from thy teat.
Wife. Well, think of marriage now. Younger than you,
  Here in Verona, ladies of esteem,   70
  Are made already mothers. By my count,
  I was your mother much upon these years

---

48 *stinted* stopped   52 *it brow* its brow   58 *say I* (a pun on 'ay' and 'I';
cf. III, ii, 45–50)   72 *much . . . years* at much the same age (indicating
that Lady Capulet's age is now twenty-eight)

45

That you are now a maid. Thus then in brief:
The valiant Paris seeks you for his love.

75 *Nurse.* A man, young lady! lady, such a man
   As all the world – why he's a man of wax.

Wife. Verona's summer hath not such a flower.

Nurse. Nay, he's a flower, in faith – a very flower.

Wife. What say you? Can you love the gentleman?

80   This night you shall behold him at our feast.
     Read o'er the volume of young Paris' face,
     And find delight writ there with beauty's pen;
     Examine every married lineament,
     And see how one another lends content;

85   And what obscured in this fair volume lies
     Find written in the margent of his eyes.
     This precious book of love, this unbound lover,
     To beautify him only lacks a cover.
     The fish lives in the sea, and 'tis much pride

90   For fair without the fair within to hide.
     That book in many's eyes doth share the glory,
     That in gold clasps locks in the golden story;
     So shall you share all that he doth possess,
     By having him making yourself no less.

95 *Nurse.* No less? Nay, bigger! Women grow by men.

Wife. Speak briefly, can you like of Paris' love?

Juliet. I'll look to like, if looking liking move;
     But no more deep will I endart mine eye
     Than your consent gives strength to make it fly.

---

76 *a man of wax* handsome, as a wax model   83 *married lineament* harmonious feature   85 *what . . . lies* i.e. his concealed inner qualities of
character   86 *margent* marginal gloss   88 *a cover* i.e. a wife   89–94 *The
fish . . . no less* i.e. as the sea enfolds the fish and the cover enfolds the book,
so you shall enfold Paris (in your arms), enhancing your good qualities
by sharing his   95 *bigger* i.e. through pregnancy   98 *endart mine eye* shoot
my eye-glance (as an arrow; cf. III, ii, 47)

Enter Servingman.

Servingman. Madam, the guests are come, supper served 100
up, you called, my young lady asked for, the nurse cursed
in the pantry, and everything in extremity. I must hence
to wait. I beseech you follow straight.

Wife. We follow thee. *[Exit Servingman.]* Juliet, the
County stays.

Nurse. Go, girl, seek happy nights to happy days. *Exeunt.* 105

❀

Enter Romeo, Mercutio, Benvolio, with five or six other I, iv
Maskers; Torchbearers.

Romeo. What, shall this speech be spoke for our excuse?
Or shall we on without apology?

Benvolio. The date is out of such prolixity.
We'll have no Cupid hoodwinked with a scarf,
Bearing a Tartar's painted bow of lath, 5
Scaring the ladies like a crowkeeper;
[Nor no without-book prologue, faintly spoke
After the prompter, for our entrance;]
But, let them measure us by what they will,
We'll measure them a measure and be gone. 10

Romeo. Give me a torch. I am not for this ambling.
Being but heavy, I will bear the light.

101–2 *cursed in the pantry* i.e. the other servants swear because the Nurse
is not helping   I, iv, 1 *this speech* (Romeo has prepared a set speech,
such as customarily introduced visiting maskers)   3 *The date . . . prolixity*
such superfluous speeches are now out of fashion   4 *hoodwinked* blindfolded   5 *Tartar's . . . lath* (the Tartar's bow, used from horseback, was
much shorter than the English longbow)   6 *crowkeeper* scarecrow   7–8
(added from Q1)   7 *without-book* memorized   8 *entrance* (pronounced
en-ter-ance)   10 *measure . . . measure* dance one dance   12 *heavy* sad,
hence 'weighted down'

Mercutio. Nay, gentle Romeo, we must have you dance.
Romeo. Not I, believe me. You have dancing shoes
15   With nimble soles; I have a soul of lead
So stakes me to the ground I cannot move.
Mercutio. You are a lover. Borrow Cupid's wings
And soar with them above a common bound.
Romeo. I am too sore enpiercèd with his shaft
20   To soar with his light feathers; and so bound
I cannot bound a pitch above dull woe.
Under love's heavy burden do I sink.
Mercutio. And, to sink in it, should you burden love –
Too great oppression for a tender thing.
25 *Romeo.* Is love a tender thing? It is too rough,
Too rude, too boist'rous, and it pricks like thorn.
Mercutio. If love be rough with you, be rough with love.
Prick love for pricking, and you beat love down.
Give me a case to put my visage in.
30   A visor for a visor! What care I
What curious eye doth quote deformities?
Here are the beetle brows shall blush for me.
Benvolio. Come, knock and enter; and no sooner in
But every man betake him to his legs.
35 *Romeo.* A torch for me! Let wantons light of heart
Tickle the senseless rushes with their heels;
For I am proverbed with a grandsire phrase,
I'll be a candle-holder and look on;
The game was ne'er so fair, and I am done.

18 *bound* a leap, required in some dances 21 *pitch* height (falconry)
30 *A visor . . . visor* a mask for a face ugly enough to be itself a mask
31 *quote* note 32 *beetle brows* beetling eyebrows (of the mask) 34 *betake
. . . legs* join the dance 36 *rushes* (used as floor coverings) 37 *grandsire
phrase* old saying 38 *candle-holder* i.e. non-participant 39 *The game . . .
done* best quit a game at the height of enjoyment (proverbial; cf. I, v, 119)

Mercutio. Tut! dun's the mouse, the constable's own
   word!   40
  If thou art Dun, we'll draw thee from the mire
  Of this sir-reverence love, wherein thou stickest
  Up to the ears. Come, we burn daylight, ho!
Romeo. Nay, that's not so.
Mercutio.   I mean, sir, in delay
  We waste our lights in vain, like lamps by day.   45
  Take our good meaning, for our judgment sits
  Five times in that ere once in our five wits.
Romeo. And we mean well in going to this masque,
  But 'tis no wit to go.
Mercutio.   Why, may one ask?
Romeo. I dreamt a dream to-night.
Mercutio.   And so did I.   50
Romeo. Well, what was yours?
Mercutio.   That dreamers often lie.
Romeo. In bed asleep, while they do dream things true.
Mercutio. O, then I see Queen Mab hath been with you.
  She is the fairies' midwife, and she comes
  In shape no bigger than an agate stone   55
  On the forefinger of an alderman,
  Drawn with a team of little atomies
  Over men's noses as they lie asleep;

---

40 *dun's the mouse* be quiet as a mouse (proverbial) *constable's own word*
i.e. the caution to be quiet 41 *Dun* (stock name for a horse) *mire* (alluding to a winter game, 'Dun is in the mire,' in which the players lifted a
heavy log representing a horse caught in the mud) 42 *sir-reverence* filthy
(literally 'save-your-reverence,' a euphemism associated with physical
functions) 43 *burn daylight* waste time (proverbial) 47 *five wits* mental
faculties: common sense (the perceptive power common to all five physical senses), fantasy, imagination, judgment (reason), memory 49 *no wit*
not intelligent 53 *Mab* (a Celtic folk name for the fairy queen) 55 *agate
stone* jewel carved with figures and set in a ring 57 *atomies* tiny creatures

Her wagon spokes made of long spinners' legs,
60 The cover, of the wings of grasshoppers;
Her traces, of the smallest spider's web;
Her collars, of the moonshine's wat'ry beams;
Her whip, of cricket's bone; the lash, of film;
Her wagoner, a small grey-coated gnat,
65 Not half so big as a round little worm
Pricked from the lazy finger of a maid;
Her chariot is an empty hazelnut,
Made by the joiner squirrel or old grub,
Time out o' mind the fairies' coachmakers.
70 And in this state she gallops night by night
Through lovers' brains, and then they dream of
        love;
O'er courtiers' knees, that dream on curtsies straight;
O'er lawyers' fingers, who straight dream on fees;
O'er ladies' lips, who straight on kisses dream,
75 Which oft the angry Mab with blisters plagues,
Because their breaths with sweetmeats tainted are.
Sometime she gallops o'er a courtier's nose,
And then dreams he of smelling out a suit;
And sometime comes she with a tithe-pig's tail
80 Tickling a parson's nose as 'a lies asleep,
Then dreams he of another benefice.
Sometimes she driveth o'er a soldier's neck,
And then dreams he of cutting foreign throats,

59 *spinners* spiders   61, 62 *traces, collars* parts of the harness   63 *film*
filament of a spider's web   65–66 *worm . . . maid* (alluding to the proverbial saying that worms breed in idle fingers)   76 *with sweetmeats* i.e. as a
result of eating sweetmeats   78 *smelling . . . suit* discovering a petitioner
who will pay for his influence with government officials   79 *tithe-pig* the
parson's tithe (tenth) of his parishioner's livestock   81 *another benefice* an
additional 'living' in the church

Of breaches, ambuscadoes, Spanish blades,
Of healths five fathom deep; and then anon   85
Drums in his ear, at which he starts and wakes,
And being thus frighted, swears a prayer or two
And sleeps again. This is that very Mab
That plats the manes of horses in the night
And bakes the elflocks in foul sluttish hairs,   90
Which once untangled much misfortune bodes.
This is the hag, when maids lie on their backs,
That presses them and learns them first to bear,
Making them women of good carriage.
This is she —

Romeo.   Peace, peace, Mercutio, peace!   95
Thou talk'st of nothing.

Mercutio.   True, I talk of dreams;
Which are the children of an idle brain,
Begot of nothing but vain fantasy;
Which is as thin of substance as the air,
And more inconstant than the wind, who woos   100
Even now the frozen bosom of the North
And, being angered, puffs away from thence,
Turning his side to the dew-dropping South.

Benvolio. This wind you talk of blows us from ourselves.
Supper is done, and we shall come too late.   105

Romeo. I fear, too early; for my mind misgives
Some consequence, yet hanging in the stars,
Shall bitterly begin his fearful date
With this night's revels and expire the term

---

85 *healths . . . deep* drinking toasts from glasses thirty feet deep   90 *elf-locks* knots of tangled hair   92 *hag* night hag, or nightmare   96 *nothing* no tangible thing   98 *fantasy* (cf. l. 47 and note)   107 *consequence* future chain of events   *hanging* (in astrology, future events are said to 'hang'— *dependere*—from the stars)

110 Of a despisèd life, closed in my breast,
     By some vile forfeit of untimely death.
     But he that hath the steerage of my course
     Direct my sail! On, lusty gentlemen!
Benvolio. Strike, drum.

I, v   *They march about the stage, and Servingmen come forth*
          with napkins.

1. Servingman. Where's Potpan, that he helps not to take
away? He shift a trencher! he scrape a trencher!

2. Servingman. When good manners shall lie all in one or
two men's hands, and they unwashed too, 'tis a foul
5   thing.

1. Servingman. Away with the joint-stools, remove the
court-cupboard, look to the plate. Good thou, save me
a piece of marchpane and, as thou loves me, let the
porter let in Susan Grindstone and Nell. *[Exit second*
10   *Servingman.]* Anthony, and Potpan!

[Enter two more Servingmen.]

3. Servingman. Ay, boy, ready.

1. Servingman. You are looked for and called for, asked
for and sought for, in the great chamber.

112 *he* God I, v, s.d. (Q2 adds 'Enter Romeo,' altered in folio to 'Enter
Servant.' It is not certain that the Maskers leave the stage at this point;
'marching about' itself sometimes signalled a change in locale.) 1, 3 *1.*
Servingman, 2. Servingman (designated 'Servingman,' '1. Servingman' in
Q2) 2 *trencher* wooden platter 3–5 *When . . . thing* (a complaint that
household decorum, 'good manners,' is sustained by too few, and too un-
tidy, servants) 6 *joint-stools* stools made by a joiner 7 *court-cupboard*
sideboard *plate* silverware 8 *marchpane* sweetmeat with almonds 9
Susan . . . Nell (girls evidently invited for a servants' party in the kitchen
after the banquet) 11, 14 *3. Servingman, 4. Servingman* (designated '2.'
and '3.' in Q2, but presumably they are Anthony and Potpan, now arrived)

4. Servingman. We cannot be here and there too. Cheerly,
  boys! Be brisk awhile, and the longer liver take all.   15
                    [Exit third and fourth Servingmen.]

*Enter [Capulet, his Wife, Juliet, Tybalt, Nurse, and] all
  the Guests and Gentlewomen to the Maskers.*

Capulet. Welcome, gentlemen! Ladies that have their toes
  Unplagued with corns will walk a bout with you.
  Ah ha, my mistresses! which of you all
  Will now deny to dance? She that makes dainty,
  She I'll swear hath corns. Am I come near ye now?   20
  Welcome, gentlemen! I have seen the day
  That I have worn a visor and could tell
  A whispering tale in a fair lady's ear,
  Such as would please. 'Tis gone, 'tis gone, 'tis gone!
  You are welcome, gentlemen! Come, musicians, play.   25
                    Music plays, and they dance.
  A hall, a hall! give room! and foot it, girls.
  More light, you knaves! and turn the tables up,
  And quench the fire, the room is grown too hot.
  Ah, sirrah, this unlooked-for sport comes well.
  Nay, sit, nay, sit, good cousin Capulet,   30
  For you and I are past our dancing days.
  How long is't now since last yourself and I
  Were in a mask?
2. Capulet.   By'r Lady, thirty years.
Capulet. What, man? 'Tis not so much, 'tis not so much;
  'Tis since the nuptial of Lucentio,   35

15 *longer . . . all* i.e. the spoils to the survivor (proverbial, but often used
in contexts like the above, advocating enjoyment of life) 17 *walk a bout*
dance a turn 19 *makes dainty* pretends to hesitate 26 *A hall* clear the
hall for dancing 29 *unlooked-for sport* (a dance was not originally planned)
33 *thirty years* (indicating Capulet's advanced age)

Come Pentecost as quickly as it will,
Some five-and-twenty years, and then we masked.

2. Capulet. 'Tis more, 'tis more. His son is elder, sir;
His son is thirty.

Capulet.   Will you tell me that?

40   His son was but a ward two years ago.

Romeo. [to a Servingman] What lady's that, which doth
   enrich the hand
Of yonder knight?

Servingman. I know not, sir.

Romeo. O, she doth teach the torches to burn bright!

45   It seems she hangs upon the cheek of night
As a rich jewel in an Ethiop's ear —
Beauty too rich for use, for earth too dear!
So shows a snowy dove trooping with crows
As yonder lady o'er her fellows shows.

50   The measure done, I'll watch her place of stand
And, touching hers, make blessèd my rude hand.
Did my heart love till now? Forswear it, sight!
For I ne'er saw true beauty till this night.

Tybalt. This, by his voice, should be a Montague.

55   Fetch me my rapier, boy. What, dares the slave
Come hither, covered with an antic face,
To fleer and scorn at our solemnity?
Now, by the stock and honor of my kin,
To strike him dead I hold it not a sin.

Capulet. Why, how now, kinsman? Wherefore storm you
60   so?

Tybalt. Uncle, this is a Montague, our foe;

---

40 *His son . . . ago* it seems only two years since his son was a minor
48 *with crows* (cf. I, ii, 89)   51 *rude* coarse-skinned   56 *antic face* comic
mask   57 *fleer* mock   *solemnity* dignified feast

A villain, that is hither come in spite
To scorn at our solemnity this night.
Capulet. Young Romeo is it?
Tybalt.   'Tis he, that villain Romeo.
Capulet. Content thee, gentle coz, let him alone.   65
'A bears him like a portly gentleman,
And, to say truth, Verona brags of him
To be a virtuous and well-governed youth.
I would not for the wealth of all this town
Here in my house do him disparagement.   70
Therefore be patient, take no note of him.
It is my will, the which if thou respect,
Show a fair presence and put off these frowns.
An ill-beseeming semblance for a feast.
Tybalt. It fits when such a villain is a guest.   75
I'll not endure him.
Capulet.   He shall be endured.
What, goodman boy! I say he shall. Go to!
Am I the master here, or you? Go to!
You'll not endure him, God shall mend my soul!
You'll make a mutiny among my guests!   80
You will set cock-a-hoop, you'll be the man!
Tybalt. Why, uncle, 'tis a shame.
Capulet.   Go to, go to!
You are a saucy boy. Is't so, indeed?
This trick may chance to scathe you. I know what.
You must contrary me! Marry, 'tis time —   85
Well said, my hearts! — You are a princox — go!

66 *portly* of good carriage   79 *God . . . soul* (an expression of impatience)
80 *mutiny* violent disturbance   81 *set cock-a-hoop* i.e. take the lead   *be the
man* play the big man   84 *scathe* injure   *what* what I'm doing   85 *'tis
time* it's time you learned your place (?)   86 *said* done   *my hearts*
(addressed to the dancers)   *princox* saucy boy

Be quiet, or – More light, more light! – For shame!
I'll make you quiet; what! – Cheerly, my hearts!
Tybalt. Patience perforce with willful choler meeting
90   Makes my flesh tremble in their different greeting.
I will withdraw; but this intrusion shall,
Now seeming sweet, convert to bitt'rest gall.   *Exit.*
Romeo. If I profane with my unworthiest hand
    This holy shrine, the gentle sin is this;
95   My lips, two blushing pilgrims, ready stand
    To smooth that rough touch with a tender kiss.
Juliet. Good pilgrim, you do wrong your hand too much,
    Which mannerly devotion shows in this;
For saints have hands that pilgrims' hands do touch,
100   And palm to palm is holy palmers' kiss.
Romeo. Have not saints lips, and holy palmers too?
Juliet. Ay, pilgrim, lips that they must use in prayer.
Romeo. O, then, dear saint, let lips do what hands do!
    They pray; grant thou, lest faith turn to despair.
105 *Juliet.* Saints do not move, though grant for prayers' sake.
Romeo. Then move not while my prayer's effect I take.
    Thus from my lips, by thine my sin is purged. *[Kisses her.]*
Juliet. Then have my lips the sin that they have took.
Romeo. Sin from my lips? O trespass sweetly urged!
    Give me my sin again.   *[Kisses her.]*
110 *Juliet.*   You kiss by th' book.
Nurse. Madam, your mother craves a word with you.

---

89 *Patience perforce* enforced self-restraint   *choler* anger   93–110 (these
lines form an English-style sonnet and the first quatrain of another)
94 *shrine* i.e. Juliet's hand   *sin* i.e. roughening her soft hand with his
coarser one (cf. l. 51)   95 *pilgrims* (so called because pilgrims visit shrines)
97–100 *Good . . . kiss* your touch is not rough, to heal it with a kiss is
unnecessary, a handclasp is sufficient greeting   100 *palmers* religious pilgrims   103 *do what hands do* i.e. press each other (in a kiss)   105 *move*
take the initiative   *grant* give permission   110 *book* book of etiquette

Romeo. What is her mother?

Nurse.   Marry, bachelor,
 Her mother is the lady of the house,
 And a good lady, and a wise and virtuous.
 I nursed her daughter that you talked withal.   115
 I tell you, he that can lay hold of her
 Shall have the chinks.

Romeo.   Is she a Capulet?
 O dear account! my life is my foe's debt.

Benvolio. Away, be gone; the sport is at the best.

Romeo. Ay, so I fear; the more is my unrest.   120

Capulet. Nay, gentlemen, prepare not to be gone;
 We have a trifling foolish banquet towards.
 Is it e'en so? Why then, I thank you all.
 I thank you, honest gentlemen. Good night.
 More torches here! Come on then, let's to bed.   125
 Ah, sirrah, by my fay, it waxes late;
 I'll to my rest.   *[Exeunt all but Juliet and Nurse.]*

Juliet. Come hither, nurse. What is yond gentleman?

Nurse. The son and heir of old Tiberio.

Juliet. What's he that now is going out of door?   130

Nurse. Marry, that, I think, be young Petruchio.

Juliet. What's he that follows there, that would not dance?

Nurse. I know not.

Juliet. Go ask his name. — If he be marrièd,
 My grave is like to be my wedding bed.   135

Nurse. His name is Romeo, and a Montague,
 The only son of your great enemy.

Juliet. My only love, sprung from my only hate!
 Too early seen unknown, and known too late!

---

115 *withal* with   117 *chinks* money   118 *my foe's debt* owed to my foe
119 *Away . . . best* (cf. I, iv, 39)   122 *banquet* light refreshments *towards*
in preparation   126 *fay* faith

57

140   Prodigious birth of love it is to me
       That I must love a loathèd enemy.
Nurse. What's this? what's this?
Juliet.   A rhyme I learnt even now
    Of one I danced withal.   *One calls within,* 'Juliet.'
Nurse.   Anon, anon!
    Come, let's away; the strangers all are gone.   *Exeunt.*

* * *

II, Cho.   *[Enter] Chorus.*

Chorus. Now old desire doth in his deathbed lie,
    And young affection gapes to be his heir;
That fair for which love groaned for and would die,
    With tender Juliet matched, is now not fair.
Now Romeo is beloved and loves again,
    Alike bewitchèd by the charm of looks;
But to his foe supposed he must complain,
    And she steal love's sweet bait from fearful hooks.
Being held a foe, he may not have access
10   To breathe such vows as lovers use to swear,
And she as much in love, her means much less
    To meet her new belovèd anywhere;
But passion lends them power, time means, to meet,
Temp'ring extremities with extreme sweet.   *[Exit.]*

* * *

140 *Prodigious* monstrous   143 *Anon* i.e. we are coming right away
II, Cho., 1 *old desire* i.e. Romeo's love of Rosaline   2 *young affection* new
love *gapes* opens his mouth hungrily   7 *complain* make a lover's plaints
8 *steal . . . hooks* (a popular conceit: the lover 'fishes' for his beloved.
For Juliet to be 'caught' is dangerous because of the family feud.)   10 *use*
are accustomed

Enter Romeo alone.

Romeo. Can I go forward when my heart is here?
Turn back, dull earth, and find thy centre out.

Enter Benvolio with Mercutio. [Romeo retires.]

Benvolio. Romeo! my cousin Romeo! Romeo!
Mercutio.   He is wise,
And, on my life, hath stol'n him home to bed.
Benvolio. He ran this way and leapt this orchard wall.   5
Call, good Mercutio.
Mercutio.   Nay, I'll conjure too.
Romeo! humors! madman! passion! lover!
Appear thou in the likeness of a sigh;
Speak but one rhyme, and I am satisfied!
Cry but 'Ay me!' pronounce but 'love' and 'dove';   10
Speak to my gossip Venus one fair word,
One nickname for her purblind son and heir
Young Abraham Cupid, he that shot so true
When King Cophetua loved the beggar maid!
He heareth not, he stirreth not, he moveth not;   15
The ape is dead, and I must conjure him.
I conjure thee by Rosaline's bright eyes,
By her high forehead and her scarlet lip,
By her fine foot, straight leg, and quivering thigh,

II, i, 1 *my heart is here* (the Neo–Platonic fancy that the heart or soul of
the lover dwells in the beloved) 2 *earth* i.e. my body *centre* i.e. my heart
or soul 6 *Nay . . . too* (printed as part of preceding speech in Q2) 7
humors whims 11 *gossip* female crony 12 *purblind* dim–sighted 13 *Young
Abraham* youthful, yet patriarchal (Cupid, or Love, was both the youngest
and the oldest of the gods) 14 *King Cophetua . . . beggar maid* (from a
popular ballad) 16 *The ape . . . him* (probably recalling a showman's
ape who 'played dead' until called with the right word-formula)

20   And the demesnes that there adjacent lie,
     That in thy likeness thou appear to us!
Benvolio. An if he hear thee, thou wilt anger him.
Mercutio. This cannot anger him. 'Twould anger him
     To raise a spirit in his mistress' circle
25   Of some strange nature, letting it there stand
     Till she had laid it and conjured it down.
     That were some spite; my invocation
     Is fair and honest: in his mistress' name,
     I conjure only but to raise up him.
Benvolio. Come, he hath hid himself among these
30   trees
     To be consorted with the humorous night.
     Blind is his love and best befits the dark.
Mercutio. If love be blind, love cannot hit the mark.
     Now will he sit under a medlar tree
35   And wish his mistress were that kind of fruit
     As maids call medlars when they laugh alone.
     O, Romeo, that she were, O that she were
     An open et cetera, thou a pop'rin pear!
     Romeo, good night. I'll to my truckle-bed;
40   This field-bed is too cold for me to sleep.
     Come, shall we go?
Benvolio.   Go then, for 'tis in vain
     To seek him here that means not to be found.

                                    Exit [with others].

II, ii *Romeo. [coming forward]* He jests at scars that never felt a
       wound.

---

20 *demesnes* domains   24 *circle* the conjurer's circle in which an evoked
spirit supposedly appears (Mercutio intends a ribald pun)   31 *humorous*
damp; also, capricious   36, 38 *medlars, pop'rin pear* fruits (used vulgarly
in reference to the sex organs)   39 *truckle-bed* trundle-bed

[Enter Juliet above at a window.]

But soft! What light through yonder window breaks?
It is the East, and Juliet is the sun!
Arise, fair sun, and kill the envious moon,
Who is already sick and pale with grief   5
That thou her maid art far more fair than she.
Be not her maid, since she is envious.
Her vestal livery is but sick and green,
And none but fools do wear it. Cast it off.
It is my lady; O, it is my love!   10
O that she knew she were!
She speaks, yet she says nothing. What of that?
Her eye discourses; I will answer it.
I am too bold; 'tis not to me she speaks.
Two of the fairest stars in all the heaven,   15
Having some business, do entreat her eyes
To twinkle in their spheres till they return.
What if her eyes were there, they in her head?
The brightness of her cheek would shame those stars
As daylight doth a lamp; her eyes in heaven   20
Would through the airy region stream so bright
That birds would sing and think it were not night.
See how she leans her cheek upon her hand!
O that I were a glove upon that hand,
That I might touch that cheek!

Juliet.   Ay me!
Romeo.   She speaks.   25
O, speak again, bright angel! for thou art

II, ii, 4 *kill* make invisible by more intense light   6 *her maid* (Diana,
moon-goddess, was patroness of virgins)   8 *vestal livery* virginity (after
Vesta, another virgin goddess)   *green* anaemic   17 *spheres* orbits

As glorious to this night, being o'er my head,
As is a wingèd messenger of heaven
Unto the white-upturnèd wond'ring eyes
30   Of mortals that fall back to gaze on him
When he bestrides the lazy-pacing clouds
And sails upon the bosom of the air.

Juliet. O Romeo, Romeo! wherefore art thou Romeo?
Deny thy father and refuse thy name;
35   Or, if thou wilt not, be but sworn my love,
And I'll no longer be a Capulet.

Romeo. [aside] Shall I hear more, or shall I speak at this?

Juliet. 'Tis but thy name that is my enemy.
Thou art thyself, though not a Montague.
40   What's Montague? It is nor hand, nor foot,
Nor arm, nor face, nor any other part
Belonging to a man. O, be some other name!
What's in a name? That which we call a rose
By any other name would smell as sweet.
45   So Romeo would, were he not Romeo called,
Retain that dear perfection which he owes
Without that title. Romeo, doff thy name;
And for thy name, which is no part of thee,
Take all myself.

Romeo.   I take thee at thy word.
50   Call me but love, and I'll be new baptized;
Henceforth I never will be Romeo.

Juliet. What man art thou that, thus bescreened in night,
So stumblest on my counsel?

Romeo.   By a name
I know not how to tell thee who I am.
55   My name, dear saint, is hateful to myself,

---

29 *white-upturnèd* (the whites show when the eyes are turned upward)
44 *name* (from Q1; Q2 reads 'word,' perhaps correctly) 46 *owes* owns

Because it is an enemy to thee.
Had I it written, I would tear the word.
Juliet. My ears have yet not drunk a hundred words
 Of thy tongue's uttering, yet I know the sound.
 Art thou not Romeo, and a Montague?   60
Romeo. Neither, fair maid, if either thee dislike.
Juliet. How camest thou hither, tell me, and wherefore?
 The orchard walls are high and hard to climb,
 And the place death, considering who thou art,
 If any of my kinsmen find thee here.   65
Romeo. With love's light wings did I o'erperch these walls;
 For stony limits cannot hold love out,
 And what love can do, that dares love attempt.
 Therefore thy kinsmen are no stop to me.
Juliet. If they do see thee, they will murder thee.   70
Romeo. Alack, there lies more peril in thine eye
 Than twenty of their swords! Look thou but sweet,
 And I am proof against their enmity.
Juliet. I would not for the world they saw thee here.
Romeo. I have night's cloak to hide me from their eyes;   75
 And but thou love me, let them find me here.
 My life were better ended by their hate
 Than death prorogued, wanting of thy love.
Juliet. By whose direction found'st thou out this place?
Romeo. By love, that first did prompt me to inquire.   80
 He lent me counsel, and I lent him eyes.
 I am no pilot; yet, wert thou as far
 As that vast shore washed with the farthest sea,
 I should adventure for such merchandise.
Juliet. Thou knowest the mask of night is on my face;   85

61 *dislike* displease   66 *o'erperch* fly over   73 *proof* armored   78 *prorogued* postponed   *wanting of* lacking   83 *farthest sea* the Pacific   84 *adventure* risk a voyage

Else would a maiden blush bepaint my cheek
For that which thou hast heard me speak to-night.
Fain would I dwell on form — fain, fain deny
What I have spoke; but farewell compliment!
90 Dost thou love me? I know thou wilt say 'Ay';
And I will take thy word. Yet, if thou swear'st,
Thou mayst prove false. At lovers' perjuries,
They say Jove laughs. O gentle Romeo,
If thou dost love, pronounce it faithfully.
95 Or if thou thinkest I am too quickly won,
I'll frown, and be perverse, and say thee nay,
So thou wilt woo; but else, not for the world.
In truth, fair Montague, I am too fond,
And therefore thou mayst think my havior light;
100 But trust me, gentleman, I'll prove more true
Than those that have more cunning to be strange.
I should have been more strange, I must confess,
But that thou overheard'st, ere I was ware,
My true-love passion. Therefore pardon me,
105 And not impute this yielding to light love,
Which the dark night hath so discoverèd.
Romeo. Lady, by yonder blessèd moon I vow,
That tips with silver all these fruit-tree tops —
Juliet. O, swear not by the moon, th' inconstant moon,
110 That monthly changes in her circled orb,
Lest that thy love prove likewise variable.
Romeo. What shall I swear by?
Juliet.   Do not swear at all;
Or if thou wilt, swear by thy gracious self,
Which is the god of my idolatry,
And I'll believe thee.

89 *compliment* etiquette   99 *havior* behavior   101 *strange* aloof, distant
103 *ware* aware of you   106 *discoverèd* revealed

64

Romeo.   If my heart's dear love —   115
Juliet. Well, do not swear. Although I joy in thee,
 I have no joy of this contract to-night.
 It is too rash, too unadvised, too sudden;
 Too like the lightning, which doth cease to be
 Ere one can say 'It lightens.' Sweet, good night!   120
 This bud of love, by summer's ripening breath,
 May prove a beauteous flow'r when next we meet.
 Good night, good night! As sweet repose and rest
 Come to thy heart as that within my breast!
Romeo. O, wilt thou leave me so unsatisfied?   125
Juliet. What satisfaction canst thou have to-night?
Romeo. Th' exchange of thy love's faithful vow for
    mine.
Juliet. I gave thee mine before thou didst request it;
 And yet I would it were to give again.
Romeo. Wouldst thou withdraw it? For what purpose,
    love?   130
Juliet. But to be frank and give it thee again.
 And yet I wish but for the thing I have.
 My bounty is as boundless as the sea,
 My love as deep; the more I give to thee,
 The more I have, for both are infinite.   135
 I hear some noise within. Dear love, adieu!
                              [Nurse calls within.]
 Anon, good nurse! Sweet Montague, be true.
 Stay but a little, I will come again.   *[Exit.]*
Romeo. O blessèd, blessèd night! I am afeard,
 Being in night, all this is but a dream,   140
 Too flattering-sweet to be substantial.

131 *frank* generous   133 *bounty* wish to give (love)   135 *The more I have*
(scholastic theologians debated how love could be given away and yet
the giver have more than before; cf. Dante, *Purgatorio*, XV, 61 ff.)

[Enter Juliet above.]

Juliet. Three words, dear Romeo, and good night indeed.
    If that thy bent of love be honorable,
    Thy purpose marriage, send me word to-morrow,
145   By one that I'll procure to come to thee,
    Where and what time thou wilt perform the rite;
    And all my fortunes at thy foot I'll lay
    And follow thee my lord throughout the world.
Nurse. *[within]* Madam!
150 *Juliet.* I come, anon. — But if thou meanest not well,
    I do beseech thee —
Nurse. *[within]* Madam!
Juliet.   By and by I come. —
    To cease thy suit and leave me to my grief.
    To-morrow will I send.
Romeo.   So thrive my soul —
155 *Juliet.* A thousand times good night!   *[Exit.]*
    Romeo. A thousand times the worse, to want thy light!
    Love goes toward love as schoolboys from their books;
    But love from love, toward school with heavy looks.

Enter Juliet [above] again.

Juliet. Hist! Romeo, hist! O for a falc'ner's voice
160   To lure this tassel-gentle back again!
    Bondage is hoarse and may not speak aloud,
    Else would I tear the cave where Echo lies
    And make her airy tongue more hoarse than mine
    With repetition of 'My Romeo!'
165 *Romeo.* It is my soul that calls upon my name.

---

143 *bent* purpose 152 *By and by* immediately 160 *tassel-gentle* tercel-gentle, or male falcon 161 *Bondage* (she feels 'imprisoned' by the nearness of her kinsmen) 165 *my soul* (cf. l. 1 and note)

How silver-sweet sound lovers' tongues by night,
Like softest music to attending ears!

Juliet. Romeo!

Romeo.   My sweet?

Juliet.   At what o'clock to-morrow
Shall I send to thee?

Romeo.   By the hour of nine.

Juliet. I will not fail. 'Tis twenty years till then.   170
I have forgot why I did call thee back.

Romeo. Let me stand here till thou remember it.

Juliet. I shall forget, to have thee still stand there,
Rememb'ring how I love thy company.

Romeo. And I'll still stay, to have thee still forget,   175
Forgetting any other home but this.

Juliet. 'Tis almost morning. I would have thee gone –
And yet no farther than a wanton's bird,
That lets it hop a little from her hand,
Like a poor prisoner in his twisted gyves,   180
And with a silken thread plucks it back again,
So loving-jealous of his liberty.

Romeo. I would I were thy bird.

Juliet.   Sweet, so would I.
Yet I should kill thee with much cherishing.
Good night, good night! Parting is such sweet sorrow   185
That I shall say good night till it be morrow.   *[Exit.]*

Romeo. Sleep dwell upon thine eyes, peace in thy breast!
Would I were sleep and peace, so sweet to rest!

---

167 *attending* paying attention   178 *wanton* spoiled child   180 *gyves* fetters
184 *cherishing* caressing   186 *morrow* morning   187–90 (In Q2 the speech
prefix 'Juliet' is mistakenly placed before the first of these lines, and they
are followed by four lines that are nearly identical with those at II, iii, 1–4.
Perhaps Shakespeare decided to let the Friar announce the dawn instead
of Romeo, and the cancelled lines in the manuscript were printed in error.)

        Hence will I to my ghostly father's cell,
190   His help to crave and my dear hap to tell.   *Exit.*

                              ❊

Enter Friar [Laurence] alone, with a basket.

    Friar. The grey-eyed morn smiles on the frowning night,
        Check'ring the Eastern clouds with streaks of light;
        And fleckèd darkness like a drunkard reels
        From forth day's path and Titan's fiery wheels.
5   Now, ere the sun advance his burning eye
        The day to cheer and night's dank dew to dry,
        I must up-fill this osier cage of ours
        With baleful weeds and precious-juicèd flowers.
        The earth that's nature's mother is her tomb.
10   What is her burying grave, that is her womb;
        And from her womb children of divers kind
        We sucking on her natural bosom find,
        Many for many virtues excellent,
        None but for some, and yet all different.
15   O, mickle is the powerful grace that lies
        In plants, herbs, stones, and their true qualities;
        For naught so vile that on the earth doth live
        But to the earth some special good doth give;
        Nor aught so good but, strained from that fair use,
20   Revolts from true birth, stumbling on abuse.
        Virtue itself turns vice, being misapplied,
        And vice sometime 's by action dignified.

---

189 *ghostly* spiritual   190 *dear hap* good luck   II, iii, 3 *fleckèd* spotted,
dappled   4 *Titan's fiery wheels* the sun's chariot wheels   7 *osier cage* willow
basket   15 *mickle* much   20 *true birth* its true nature   22 *dignified* made
worthy

Enter Romeo.

Within the infant rind of this weak flower
Poison hath residence, and medicine power;
For this, being smelt, with that part cheers each part;   25
Being tasted, slays all senses with the heart.
Two such opposèd kings encamp them still
In man as well as herbs — grace and rude will;
And where the worser is predominant,
Full soon the canker death eats up that plant.   30
Romeo. Good morrow, father.
Friar.   Benedicite!
What early tongue so sweet saluteth me?
Young son, it argues a distemperèd head
So soon to bid good morrow to thy bed.
Care keeps his watch in every old man's eye,   35
And where care lodges, sleep will never lie;
But where unbruisèd youth with unstuffed brain
Doth couch his limbs, there golden sleep doth reign.
Therefore thy earliness doth me assure
Thou art uproused with some distemp'rature;   40
Or if not so, then here I hit it right —
Our Romeo hath not been in bed to-night.
Romeo. That last is true — the sweeter rest was mine.
Friar. God pardon sin! Wast thou with Rosaline?
Romeo. With Rosaline, my ghostly father? No.   45
I have forgot that name and that name's woe.
Friar. That's my good son! But where hast thou been then?
Romeo. I'll tell thee ere thou ask it me again.

22 S.D. (This entrance seems premature, but cf. entrance of Nurse at
III, iii, 70) 25–26 *being* . . . *heart* i.e. being smelt, stimulates; being tasted,
kills 27 *still* always 28 *grace* power of goodness *rude will* coarse impulses
of the flesh 30 *canker* the worm in the bud 31 *morrow* morning *Benedicite* bless you 37 *unstuffed* carefree

69

I have been feasting with mine enemy,
50   Where on a sudden one hath wounded me
That's by me wounded. Both our remedies
Within thy help and holy physic lies.
I bear no hatred, blessèd man, for, lo,
My intercession likewise steads my foe. ❧

55 *Friar.* Be plain, good son, and homely in thy drift.
Riddling confession finds but riddling shrift.
    Romeo. Then plainly know my heart's dear love is set
On the fair daughter of rich Capulet;
As mine on hers, so hers is set on mine,
60   And all combined, save what thou must combine
By holy marriage. When, and where, and how
We met, we wooed, and made exchange of vow,
I'll tell thee as we pass; but this I pray,
That thou consent to marry us to-day.

65 *Friar.* Holy Saint Francis! What a change is here!
Is Rosaline, that thou didst love so dear,
So soon forsaken? Young men's love then lies
Not truly in their hearts, but in their eyes.
Jesu Maria! What a deal of brine
70   Hath washed thy sallow cheeks for Rosaline!
How much salt water thrown away in waste
To season love, that of it doth not taste!
The sun not yet thy sighs from heaven clears,
Thy old groans ring yet in mine ancient ears.
75   Lo, here upon thy cheek the stain doth sit
Of an old tear that is not washed off yet.
If e'er thou wast thyself, and these woes thine,
Thou and these woes were all for Rosaline.

---

52 *physic* medicine   54 *intercession* request   *steads* benefits   55 *homely*
simple   *drift* explanation   56 *shrift* absolution   72 *season* flavor   *doth not
taste* i.e. now has no savor

And art thou changed? Pronounce this sentence then:
Women may fall when there's no strength in men.   80
Romeo. Thou chid'st me oft for loving Rosaline.
Friar. For doting, not for loving, pupil mine.
Romeo. And bad'st me bury love.
Friar.   Not in a grave
To lay one in, another out to have.
Romeo. I pray thee chide not. She whom I love now   85
Doth grace for grace and love for love allow.
The other did not so.
Friar.   O, she knew well
Thy love did read by rote, that could not spell.
But come, young waverer, come go with me.
In one respect I'll thy assistant be;   90
For this alliance may so happy prove
To turn your households' rancor to pure love.
Romeo. O, let us hence! I stand on sudden haste.
Friar. Wisely and slow. They stumble that run fast.
                                        Exeunt.

✤

Enter Benvolio and Mercutio.   II, iv

Mercutio. Where the devil should this Romeo be?
Came he not home to-night?
Benvolio. Not to his father's. I spoke with his man.
Mercutio. Why, that same pale hard-hearted wench, that
    Rosaline,
Torments him so that he will sure run mad.   5
Benvolio. Tybalt, the kinsman to old Capulet,
Hath sent a letter to his father's house.

80 *strength* constancy 86 *grace* favor 88 *by rote . . . spell* like a child
repeating words without understanding them 93 *on* in need of

Mercutio. A challenge, on my life.

Benvolio. Romeo will answer it.

10 *Mercutio.* Any man that can write may answer a letter.

Benvolio. Nay, he will answer the letter's master, how he
dares, being dared.

Mercutio. Alas, poor Romeo, he is already dead! stabbed
with a white wench's black eye; run through the ear
15 with a love song; the very pin of his heart cleft with the
blind bow-boy's butt-shaft; and is he a man to encounter
Tybalt?

Benvolio. Why, what is Tybalt?

Mercutio. More than Prince of Cats, I can tell you. O, he's
20 the courageous captain of compliments. He fights as you
sing pricksong – keeps time, distance, and proportion;
he rests his minim rests, one, two, and the third in your
bosom! the very butcher of a silk button, a duellist, a
duellist! a gentleman of the very first house, of the first
25 and second cause. Ah, the immortal passado! the punto
reverso! the hay!

Benvolio. The what?

Mercutio. The pox of such antic, lisping, affecting fantasticoes – these new tuners of accent! 'By Jesu, a very good
30 blade! a very tall man! a very good whore!' Why, is not

II, iv, 15 *pin* peg in the centre of a target, bull's-eye 16 *bow-boy's butt-
shaft* Cupid's arrow (jestingly identified as a barbless target-arrow) 16–17
is . . . Tybalt (Mercutio has doubts of Romeo's prowess while he is
despondent and low-spirited) 19 *Prince of Cats* (Tybalt, or Tybert, is the
cat's name in mediaeval stories of Reynard the Fox) 20 *compliments*
etiquette 21 *pricksong* written music 22 *minim rests* shortest rests (in the
old musical notation) *third* third rapier thrust 23 *button* i.e. on his
opponent's shirt 24 *first house* finest fencing school 24–25 *first and second
cause* causes for a challenge (in the duellist's code) 25 *passado* lunge
25–26 *punto reverso* backhanded stroke 26 *hay* home-thrust (from *hai*,
'I have it'; a new term to Benvolio) 28–29 *fantasticoes* coxcombs 30 *tall*
brave

this a lamentable thing, grandsir, that we should be thus
afflicted with these strange flies, these fashion-mongers,
these pardon-me's, who stand so much on the new form
that they cannot sit at ease on the old bench? O, their
bones, their bones!   35

Enter Romeo.

Benvolio. Here comes Romeo! here comes Romeo!

Mercutio. Without his roe, like a dried herring. O flesh,
flesh, how art thou fishified! Now is he for the numbers
that Petrarch flowed in. Laura, to his lady, was a
kitchen wench (marry, she had a better love to berhyme   40
her), Dido a dowdy, Cleopatra a gypsy, Helen and Hero
hildings and harlots, Thisbe a grey eye or so, but not to
the purpose. Signior Romeo, bon jour! There's a French
salutation to your French slop. You gave us the counter-
feit fairly last night.   45

Romeo. Good morrow to you both. What counterfeit did
I give you?

Mercutio. The slip, sir, the slip. Can you not conceive?

Romeo. Pardon, good Mercutio. My business was great,
and in such a case as mine a man may strain courtesy.   50

Mercutio. That's as much as to say, such a case as yours
constrains a man to bow in the hams.

Romeo. Meaning, to curtsy.

31 *grandsir* good sir   33 *pardon-me's* i.e. sticklers for etiquette   *form* (1)
fashion (2) school-bench   34 *old bench* i.e. native manners and learning
35 *bones* 'bon's' (Fr. 'good's')   37 *Without his roe* i.e. 'shot'   38 *numbers*
verses   39 *Laura* Petrarch's beloved   *to* in comparison with   41 *Dido*
Queen of Carthage who fell in love with Aeneas   *Helen* Helen of Troy
Hero beloved of Leander   42 *hildings* worthless creatures   *Thisbe* (Pyramus
and Thisbe were young lovers whose story resembles that of Romeo and
Juliet)   42–43 *not to the purpose* not worth mentioning   43 *bon jour* good
day   44 *slop* trousers   45 *fairly* effectively   48 *slip* (1) escape (2) counterfeit coin   51 *such . . . yours* the pox (implied)   52 *hams* hips

73

Mercutio. Thou hast most kindly hit it.

55 *Romeo.* A most courteous exposition.

Mercutio. Nay, I am the very pink of courtesy.

Romeo. Pink for flower.

Mercutio. Right.

Romeo. Why, then is my pump well-flowered.

60 *Mercutio.* Sure wit, follow me this jest now till thou hast
worn out thy pump, that, when the single sole of it is
worn, the jest may remain, after the wearing, solely
singular.

Romeo. O single-soled jest, solely singular for the single-
65 ness!

Mercutio. Come between us, good Benvolio! My wits faint.

Romeo. Swits and spurs, swits and spurs! or I'll cry a match.

Mercutio. Nay, if our wits run the wild-goose chase, I am
done; for thou hast more of the wild goose in one of thy
70 wits than, I am sure, I have in my whole five. Was I
with you there for the goose?

Romeo. Thou wast never with me for anything when thou
wast not there for the goose.

Mercutio. I will bite thee by the ear for that jest.

75 *Romeo.* Nay, good goose, bite not!

Mercutio. Thy wit is a very bitter sweeting; it is a most
sharp sauce.

---

54 *kindly hit it* interpreted it in your own way   57 *flower* ('flower of
courtesy' was the usual complimentary form; cf. II, v, 43)   59 *pump* shoe
well-flowered (because pinked, or punched, with an ornamental design)
62–63 *solely singular* uniquely remarkable   64 *single-soled* weak   64–65
singleness weakness   66 *My wits faint* my mind fails in this intricate word
play   67 *Swits and spurs* switches and spurs, i.e. keep your horse (wit)
running *cry a match* claim victory   68 *wild-goose chase* cross-country horse
race of 'follow the leader'   70–71 *Was . . . goose* was I accurate in calling
you a goose   72–73 *Thou . . . goose* you were never in my company for
any purpose when you weren't looking for a prostitute (goose)   75 *good
. . . not* spare me (proverbial)   76 *bitter sweeting* a tart species of apple

Romeo. And is it not, then, well served in to a sweet goose?

Mercutio. O, here's a wit of cheveril, that stretches from
an inch narrow to an ell broad!   80

Romeo. I stretch it out for that word 'broad,' which, added
to the goose, proves thee far and wide a broad goose.

Mercutio. Why, is not this better now than groaning for
love? Now art thou sociable, now art thou Romeo; now
art thou what thou art, by art as well as by nature. For   85
this drivelling love is like a great natural that runs lolling
up and down to hide his bauble in a hole.

Benvolio. Stop there, stop there!

Mercutio. Thou desirest me to stop in my tale against the
hair.   90

Benvolio. Thou wouldst else have made thy tale large.

Mercutio. O, thou art deceived! I would have made it short;
for I was come to the whole depth of my tale, and meant
indeed to occupy the argument no longer.

Romeo. Here's goodly gear!   95

Enter Nurse and her Man [Peter].

Mercutio. A sail, a sail!

Benvolio. Two, two! a shirt and a smock.

Nurse. Peter!

Peter. Anon.

Nurse. My fan, Peter.   100

Mercutio. Good Peter, to hide her face; for her fan's the
fairer face.

Nurse. God ye good morrow, gentlemen.

78 *sweet* tasty, tender   79 *cheveril* kid-skin, easily stretched   80 *ell* 45
inches (English measure)   82 *broad goose* possibly, a goose from the
Broads, shallow Norfolk lakes (?)   86 *natural* idiot   87 *bauble* jester's
wand, here a phallic symbol   89–90 *against the hair* with my hair rubbed
the wrong way, against my inclination   91 *large* broad, indecent   94
occupy the argument pursue the subject   95 *gear* stuff   97 *shirt, smock* male
and female garments

Mercutio. God ye good-den, fair gentlewoman.

105 *Nurse.* Is it good-den?

Mercutio. 'Tis no less, I tell ye; for the bawdy hand of the
   dial is now upon the prick of noon.

Nurse. Out upon you! What a man are you!

Romeo. One, gentlewoman, that God hath made for him-
110   self to mar.

Nurse. By my troth, it is well said. 'For himself to mar,'
   quoth 'a? Gentlemen, can any of you tell me where I
   may find the young Romeo?

Romeo. I can tell you; but young Romeo will be older
115   when you have found him than he was when you sought
   him. I am the youngest of that name, for fault of a worse.

Nurse. You say well.

Mercutio. Yea, is the worst well? Very well took, i' faith!
   wisely, wisely.

120 *Nurse.* If you be he, sir, I desire some confidence with you.

Benvolio. She will endite him to some supper.

Mercutio. A bawd, a bawd, a bawd! So ho!

Romeo. What hast thou found?

Mercutio. No hare, sir; unless a hare, sir, in a lenten pie,
125   that is something stale and hoar ere it be spent.

[He walks by them and sings.]

An old hare hoar,
And an old hare hoar,
Is very good meat in Lent;

---

105 *Is it good-den* is it already afternoon   107 *prick* (1) indented point on
a clock-face or sundial (2) phallus   112 *quoth 'a* said he   116 *for . . . worse*
(parodying 'for want of a better')   118 *took* understood   120 *confidence*
conference (malapropism)   121 *endite* invite (anticipating a malapropism)
122 *So ho* (hunter's cry on sighting game)   124 *hare* i.e. prostitute   *lenten*
pie meat pie eaten sparingly during Lent   125 *hoar* (1) grey with mould
(2) grey-haired, with wordplay on 'whore'   125 s.d. (from Q1)

> But a hare that is hoar
> Is too much for a score   130
> When it hoars ere it be spent.

Romeo, will you come to your father's? We'll to dinner
thither.

Romeo. I will follow you.

Mercutio. Farewell, ancient lady. Farewell,   135
    [*sings*] lady, lady, lady.   *Exeunt [Mercutio, Benvolio].*

Nurse. I pray you, sir, what saucy merchant was this that
    was so full of his ropery?

Romeo. A gentleman, nurse, that loves to hear himself talk
    and will speak more in a minute than he will stand to in   140
    a month.

Nurse. An 'a speak anything against me, I'll take him down,
    an 'a were lustier than he is, and twenty such Jacks; and
    if I cannot, I'll find those that shall. Scurvy knave! I am
    none of his flirt-gills; I am none of his skains-mates. And 145
    thou must stand by too, and suffer every knave to use me
    at his pleasure!

Peter. I saw no man use you at his pleasure. If I had, my
    weapon should quickly have been out, I warrant you. I
    dare draw as soon as another man, if I see occasion in a   150
    good quarrel, and the law on my side.

Nurse. Now, afore God, I am so vexed that every part about
    me quivers. Scurvy knave! Pray you, sir, a word; and,
    as I told you, my young lady bid me inquire you out.
    What she bid me say, I will keep to myself; but first let   155
    me tell ye, if ye should lead her into a fool's paradise, as
    they say, it were a very gross kind of behavior, as they

136 *lady, lady, lady* (ballad refrain from *Chaste Susanna*)   138 *ropery*
vulgar jesting   145 *flirt-gills* flirting Jills   *skains-mates* outlaws, gangster
molls   148–49 *my weapon . . . out* (cf. I, i, 30 and note)   156 *lead . . .
paradise* seduce her (proverbial)

say; for the gentlewoman is young; and therefore, if you
should deal double with her, truly it were an ill thing to
160   be offered to any gentlewoman, and very weak dealing.

Romeo. Nurse, commend me to thy lady and mistress. I
    protest unto thee —

Nurse. Good heart, and i' faith I will tell her as much. Lord,
    Lord! she will be a joyful woman.

165 *Romeo.* What wilt thou tell her, nurse? Thou dost not
    mark me.

Nurse. I will tell her, sir, that you do protest, which, as I
    take it, is a gentlemanlike offer.

Romeo. Bid her devise
170   Some means to come to shrift this afternoon;
    And there she shall at Friar Laurence' cell
    Be shrived and married. Here is for thy pains.

Nurse. No, truly, sir; not a penny.

Romeo. Go to! I say you shall.

175 *Nurse.* This afternoon, sir? Well, she shall be there.

Romeo. And stay, good nurse, behind the abbey wall.
    Within this hour my man shall be with thee
    And bring thee cords made like a tackled stair,
    Which to the high topgallant of my joy
180   Must be my convoy in the secret night.
    Farewell. Be trusty, and I'll quit thy pains.
    Farewell. Commend me to thy mistress.

Nurse. Now God in heaven bless thee! Hark you, sir.

Romeo. What say'st thou, my dear nurse?

185 *Nurse.* Is your man secret? Did you ne'er hear say,
    Two may keep counsel, putting one away?

Romeo. I warrant thee my man's as true as steel.

---

160 *weak* unmanly 178 *tackled stair* rope ladder 179 *topgallant* mast and
sail above the mainmast 180 *convoy* conveyance 181 *quit thy pains*
reward your efforts

Nurse. Well, sir, my mistress is the sweetest lady. Lord,
Lord! when 'twas a little prating thing – O, there is a
nobleman in town, one Paris, that would fain lay knife   190
aboard; but she, good soul, had as lieve see a toad, a
very toad, as see him. I anger her sometimes, and tell her
that Paris is the properer man; but I'll warrant you, when
I say so, she looks as pale as any clout in the versal world.
Doth not rosemary and Romeo begin both with a letter?   195

Romeo. Ay, nurse; what of that? Both with an R.

Nurse. Ah, mocker! that's the dog's name. R is for the –
No; I know it begins with some other letter; and she
hath the prettiest sententious of it, of you and rosemary,
that it would do you good to hear it.   200

Romeo. Commend me to thy lady.

Nurse. Ay, a thousand times. *[Exit Romeo.]* Peter!

Peter. Anon.

Nurse. [Peter, take my fan, and go] before, and apace.
                                    Exit [after Peter].

※

                    Enter Juliet.   II, v

Juliet. The clock struck nine when I did send the nurse;
  In half an hour she promised to return.
  Perchance she cannot meet him. That's not so.
  O, she is lame! Love's heralds should be thoughts,
  Which ten times faster glide than the sun's beams   5
  Driving back shadows over low'ring hills.

190–91 *lay knife aboard* i.e. partake of this dish   191 *lieve* willingly
194 *clout* cloth   *versal* universal   197 *dog's name* (R was called 'the dog's
letter,' since the sound r-r-r-r supposedly resembles a dog's growl. The
Nurse thinks it an ugly sound.)   199 *sententious* sentences   204 *Peter . . .
go* (from Q1)

Therefore do nimble-pinioned doves draw Love,
And therefore hath the wind-swift Cupid wings.
Now is the sun upon the highmost hill
10   Of this day's journey, and from nine till twelve
Is three long hours; yet she is not come.
Had she affections and warm youthful blood,
She would be as swift in motion as a ball;
My words would bandy her to my sweet love,
15   And his to me.
But old folks, many feign as they were dead —
Unwieldy, slow, heavy and pale as lead.

Enter Nurse [and Peter].

O God, she comes! O honey nurse, what news?
Hast thou met with him? Send thy man away.
20   *Nurse.* Peter, stay at the gate.   *[Exit Peter.]*
Juliet. Now, good sweet nurse — O Lord, why lookest thou
        sad?
Though news be sad, yet tell them merrily;
If good, thou shamest the music of sweet news
By playing it to me with so sour a face.
25   *Nurse.* I am aweary, give me leave awhile.
Fie, how my bones ache! What a jaunce have I had!
Juliet. I would thou hadst my bones, and I thy news.
Nay, come, I pray thee speak. Good, good nurse, speak.
Nurse. Jesu, what haste! Can you not stay awhile?
30   Do you not see that I am out of breath?
Juliet. How art thou out of breath when thou hast breath

II, v, 7 *nimble-pinioned* swift-winged   *doves* (Venus' birds, who draw her
chariot) 9 *upon . . . hill* at the zenith   14 *bandy* speed, as in tennis   16 *old
. . . dead* many persons speak figuratively of old folks as being dead   25 *give
me leave* let me alone   26 *jaunce* jolting   29 *stay* wait

To say to me that thou art out of breath?
The excuse that thou dost make in this delay
Is longer than the tale thou dost excuse.
Is thy news good or bad? Answer to that.   35
Say either, and I'll stay the circumstance.
Let me be satisfied, is't good or bad?

Nurse. Well, you have made a simple choice; you know
not how to choose a man. Romeo? No, not he. Though
his face be better than any man's, yet his leg excels all 40
men's; and for a hand and a foot, and a body, though
they be not to be talked on, yet they are past compare. He
is not the flower of courtesy, but, I'll warrant him, as
gentle as a lamb. Go thy ways, wench; serve God. What,
have you dined at home?   45

Juliet. No, no. But all this did I know before.
What says he of our marriage? What of that?

Nurse. Lord, how my head aches! What a head have I!
It beats as it would fall in twenty pieces.
My back a t' other side – ah, my back, my back!   50
Beshrew your heart for sending me about
To catch my death with jauncing up and down!

Juliet. I' faith, I am sorry that thou art not well.
Sweet, sweet, sweet nurse, tell me, what says my love?

Nurse. Your love says, like an honest gentleman, and a 55
courteous, and a kind, and a handsome, and, I warrant,
a virtuous – Where is your mother?

Juliet. Where is my mother? Why, she is within.
Where should she be? How oddly thou repliest!
'Your love says, like an honest gentleman,   60
"Where is your mother?"'

Nurse.   O God's Lady dear!

36 *stay the circumstance* wait for details   38 *simple* foolish   50 *a* on   51
Beshrew shame on

81

Are you so hot? Marry come up, I trow.
Is this the poultice for my aching bones?
Henceforward do your messages yourself.
65 *Juliet.* Here's such a coil! Come, what says Romeo?
Nurse. Have you got leave to go to shrift to-day?
Juliet. I have.
Nurse. Then hie you hence to Friar Laurence' cell;
There stays a husband to make you a wife.
70 Now comes the wanton blood up in your cheeks:
They'll be in scarlet straight at any news.
Hie you to church; I must another way,
To fetch a ladder, by the which your love
Must climb a bird's nest soon when it is dark.
75 I am the drudge, and toil in your delight;
But you shall bear the burden soon at night.
Go; I'll to dinner; hie you to the cell.
Juliet. Hie to high fortune! Honest nurse, farewell. *Exeunt.*

❦

II, vi   *Enter Friar [Laurence] and Romeo.*

Friar. So smile the heavens upon this holy act
That after-hours with sorrow chide us not!
Romeo. Amen, amen! But come what sorrow can,
It cannot countervail the exchange of joy
5 That one short minute gives me in her sight.
Do thou but close our hands with holy words,
Then love-devouring death do what he dare —
It is enough I may but call her mine.

---

62 *hot* angry *Marry come up* by the Virgin Mary, take your come-uppance
(penalty) *trow* trust 65 *coil* fuss 71 *in scarlet* (Juliet blushes easily—cf.
II, ii, 86; III, ii, 14) *straight* straightway 74 *climb . . . nest* i.e. climb to
Juliet's room II, vi, 4 *countervail* outweigh

Friar. These violent delights have violent ends
  And in their triumph die, like fire and powder, 10
  Which, as they kiss, consume. The sweetest honey
  Is loathsome in his own deliciousness
  And in the taste confounds the appetite.
  Therefore love moderately: long love doth so;
  Too swift arrives as tardy as too slow. 15

Enter Juliet.

  Here comes the lady. O, so light a foot
  Will ne'er wear out the everlasting flint.
  A lover may bestride the gossamer
  That idles in the wanton summer air,
  And yet not fall; so light is vanity. 20
Juliet. Good even to my ghostly confessor.
Friar. Romeo shall thank thee, daughter, for us both.
Juliet. As much to him, else is his thanks too much.
Romeo. Ah, Juliet, if the measure of thy joy
  Be heaped like mine, and that thy skill be more 25
  To blazon it, then sweeten with thy breath
  This neighbor air, and let rich music's tongue
  Unfold the imagined happiness that both
  Receive in either by this dear encounter.
Juliet. Conceit, more rich in matter than in words, 30
  Brags of his substance, not of ornament.
  They are but beggars that can count their worth;

12 *Is loathsome* i.e. if eaten to excess 15 *Too . . . slow* (proverbial; cf.
II, iii, 94) 17 *wear . . . flint* (suggested by the proverb 'In time small
water drops will wear away the stone') 18 *gossamer* spider's web 20 *vanity* transitory earthly love (cf. Ecclesiastes 9:9) 21 *ghostly* spiritual 23 *As
much* the same greeting 25 *that* if *thy . . . more* you sing better than I
26 *blazon* set forth 30-31 *Conceit . . . ornament* my understanding is fixed
upon the reality of my great love, not upon a vocal expression of it

But my true love is grown to such excess
I cannot sum up sum of half my wealth.

35 *Friar.* Come, come with me, and we will make short work;
For, by your leaves, you shall not stay alone
Till Holy Church incorporate two in one.   *[Exeunt.]*

❦

              Enter Mercutio, Benvolio, and Men.

Benvolio. I pray thee, good Mercutio, let's retire.
The day is hot, the Capulets abroad,
And, if we meet, we shall not 'scape a brawl,
For now, these hot days, is the mad blood stirring.

5 *Mercutio.* Thou art like one of these fellows that, when he
enters the confines of a tavern, claps me his sword upon
the table and says 'God send me no need of thee!' and
by the operation of the second cup draws him on the
drawer, when indeed there is no need.

10 *Benvolio.* Am I like such a fellow?

Mercutio. Come, come, thou art as hot a Jack in thy mood
as any in Italy; and as soon moved to be moody, and as
soon moody to be moved.

Benvolio. And what to?

15 *Mercutio.* Nay, an there were two such, we should have
none shortly, for one would kill the other. Thou! why,
thou wilt quarrel with a man that hath a hair more or a
hair less in his beard than thou hast. Thou wilt quarrel
with a man for cracking nuts, having no other reason
20 but because thou hast hazel eyes. What eye but such an

---

33 *love . . . excess* (cf. II, ii, 135 and note)   III, i, 8–9 *by the operation . . .
drawer* after drinking only two cups of wine, draws his sword against the
waiter   12 *moody* angry

84

eye would spy out such a quarrel? Thy head is as full of
quarrels as an egg is full of meat; and yet thy head hath
been beaten as addle as an egg for quarrelling. Thou hast
quarrelled with a man for coughing in the street, because
he hath wakened thy dog that hath lain asleep in the sun. 25
Didst thou not fall out with a tailor for wearing his new
doublet before Easter? with another for tying his new
shoes with old riband? And yet thou wilt tutor me from
quarrelling!

Benvolio. An I were so apt to quarrel as thou art, any man 30
should buy the fee simple of my life for an hour and a
quarter.

Mercutio. The fee simple? O simple!

Enter Tybalt and others.

Benvolio. By my head, here come the Capulets.

Mercutio. By my heel, I care not. 35

Tybalt. Follow me close, for I will speak to them.
Gentlemen, good-den. A word with one of you.

Mercutio. And but one word with one of us?
Couple it with something; make it a word and a blow.

Tybalt. You shall find me apt enough to that, sir, an you 40
will give me occasion.

Mercutio. Could you not take some occasion without
giving?

Tybalt. Mercutio, thou consortest with Romeo.

Mercutio. Consort? What, dost thou make us minstrels? 45
An thou make minstrels of us, look to hear nothing but

21 *spy out* see occasion for   27 *doublet* jacket   28 *riband* ribbon   31 *fee
simple* permanent lease   31–32 *hour and a quarter* probable duration of the
lease, i.e. of my life   33 *O simple* O stupid   33 S.D. (Q2 includes the name
'Petruchio')   37 *good-den* good afternoon   45 *Consort* (1) associate with
(2) accompany in vocal or instrumental music   *minstrels* (a more disrepu-
table title than 'musicians'; cf. IV, v, 111–12)

discords. Here's my fiddlestick; here's that shall make
you dance. Zounds, consort!
Benvolio. We talk here in the public haunt of men.
50   Either withdraw unto some private place,
Or reason coldly of your grievances,
Or else depart. Here all eyes gaze on us.
Mercutio. Men's eyes were made to look, and let them gaze.
I will not budge for no man's pleasure, I.

Enter Romeo.

55 Tybalt. Well, peace be with you, sir. Here comes my man.
Mercutio. But I'll be hanged, sir, if he wear your livery.
Marry, go before to field, he'll be your follower!
Your worship in that sense may call him man.
Tybalt. Romeo, the love I bear thee can afford
60   No better term than this: thou art a villain.
Romeo. Tybalt, the reason that I have to love thee
Doth much excuse the appertaining rage
To such a greeting. Villain am I none.
Therefore farewell. I see thou knowest me not.
65 Tybalt. Boy, this shall not excuse the injuries
That thou hast done me; therefore turn and draw.
Romeo. I do protest I never injured thee,
But love thee better than thou canst devise
Till thou shalt know the reason of my love;
70   And so, good Capulet, which name I tender
As dearly as mine own, be satisfied.
Mercutio. O calm, dishonorable, vile submission!

---

47 *fiddlestick* i.e. rapier   48 *Zounds* by God's wounds   56 *livery* servant's
uniform ('my man' could mean 'my manservant')   57 *field* duelling ground
62 *appertaining rage* suitably angry reaction   68 *devise* understand   70
tender value

Alla stoccata carries it away.   *[Draws.]*
Tybalt, you ratcatcher, will you walk?
Tybalt. What wouldst thou have with me?   75
Mercutio. Good King of Cats, nothing but one of your
  nine lives. That I mean to make bold withal, and, as you
  shall use me hereafter, dry-beat the rest of the eight. Will
  you pluck your sword out of his pilcher by the ears?
  Make haste, lest mine be about your ears ere it be out.   80
Tybalt. I am for you.   *[Draws.]*
Romeo. Gentle Mercutio, put thy rapier up.
Mercutio. Come, sir, your passado!   *[They fight.]*
Romeo. Draw, Benvolio; beat down their weapons.
  Gentlemen, for shame! forbear this outrage!   85
  Tybalt, Mercutio, the Prince expressly hath
  Forbid this bandying in Verona streets.
  Hold, Tybalt! Good Mercutio!
      [Tybalt under Romeo's arm thrusts Mercutio in, and flies
                          with his Followers.]
Mercutio.   I am hurt.
  A plague a both your houses! I am sped.
  Is he gone and hath nothing?
Benvolio.   What, art thou hurt?   90
Mercutio. Ay, ay, a scratch, a scratch. Marry, 'tis enough.
  Where is my page? Go, villain, fetch a surgeon.
                          [Exit Page.]
Romeo. Courage, man. The hurt cannot be much.
Mercutio. No, 'tis not so deep as a well, nor so wide as a
  church door; but 'tis enough, 'twill serve. Ask for me   95
  to-morrow, and you shall find me a grave man. I am

73 *Alla stoccata* 'at the thrust'; i.e. Tybalt *carries it away* triumphs, gets
away with it   77 *nine lives* (proverbial: a cat has nine lives)   78 *dry-beat*
thrash   79 *pilcher* scabbard   83 *passado* lunge   88 s.d. (from Q1; Q2
reads 'Away Tybalt.')   89 *a* on   *sped* mortally wounded   96 *grave* (1)
serious (2) inhabiting the grave

peppered, I warrant, for this world. A plague a both
your houses! Zounds, a dog, a rat, a mouse, a cat, to
scratch a man to death! a braggart, a rogue, a villain,
100 that fights by the book of arithmetic! Why the devil came
you between us? I was hurt under your arm.
Romeo. I thought all for the best.
Mercutio. Help me into some house, Benvolio,
Or I shall faint. A plague a both your houses!
105 They have made worms' meat of me. I have it,
And soundly too. Your houses!

Exit, [supported by Benvolio].

Romeo. This gentleman, the Prince's near ally,
My very friend, hath got this mortal hurt
In my behalf — my reputation stained
110 With Tybalt's slander — Tybalt, that an hour
Hath been my cousin. O sweet Juliet,
Thy beauty hath made me effeminate
And in my temper soft'ned valor's steel!

Enter Benvolio.

Benvolio. O Romeo, Romeo, brave Mercutio is dead!
115 That gallant spirit hath aspired the clouds,
Which too untimely here did scorn the earth.
Romeo. This day's black fate on moe days doth depend;
This but begins the woe others must end.

[Enter Tybalt.]

Benvolio. Here comes the furious Tybalt back again.
120 *Romeo.* Alive in triumph, and Mercutio slain?

100 *by . . . arithmetic* by timing his strokes (cf. II, iv, 21) 105 *worms'
meat* i.e. a corpse *I have it* I am wounded 108 *very* true 115 *aspired*
climbed **toward** 117 *moe* more *depend* hang down over (cf. I, iv, 107
and note)

Away to heaven respective lenity,
And fire-eyed fury be my conduct now!
Now, Tybalt, take the 'villain' back again
That late thou gavest me; for Mercutio's soul
Is but a little way above our heads,   125
Staying for thine to keep him company.
Either thou or I, or both, must go with him.

Tybalt. Thou, wretched boy, that didst consort him here,
Shalt with him hence.

Romeo.   This shall determine that.

                              They fight. Tybalt falls.

Benvolio. Romeo, away, be gone!   130
The citizens are up, and Tybalt slain.
Stand not amazed. The Prince will doom thee death
If thou art taken. Hence, be gone, away!

Romeo. O, I am fortune's fool!

Benvolio.   Why dost thou stay?

                              Exit Romeo.

                    Enter Citizens.

Citizen. Which way ran he that killed Mercutio?   135
Tybalt, that murderer, which way ran he?

Benvolio. There lies that Tybalt.

Citizen.   Up, sir, go with me.
I charge thee in the Prince's name obey.

    *Enter Prince [attended], old Montague, Capulet, their
        Wives, and all.*

Prince. Where are the vile beginners of this fray?

Benvolio. O noble Prince, I can discover all   140

---

121 *respective lenity* reasoned gentleness (personified as an angel)   122 *fire-
eyed fury* (fury personified)   *conduct* guide   134 *fool* dupe, victim   140
discover reveal

The unlucky manage of this fatal brawl.
There lies the man, slain by young Romeo,
That slew thy kinsman, brave Mercutio.

Capulet's Wife. Tybalt, my cousin! O my brother's child!
145   O Prince! O husband! O, the blood is spilled
Of my dear kinsman! Prince, as thou art true,
For blood of ours shed blood of Montague.
O cousin, cousin!

Prince. Benvolio, who began this bloody fray?

150 *Benvolio.* Tybalt, here slain, whom Romeo's hand did slay.
Romeo, that spoke him fair, bid him bethink
How nice the quarrel was, and urged withal
Your high displeasure. All this — utterèd
With gentle breath, calm look, knees humbly bowed —
155   Could not take truce with the unruly spleen
Of Tybalt deaf to peace, but that he tilts
With piercing steel at bold Mercutio's breast;
Who, all as hot, turns deadly point to point,
And, with a martial scorn, with one hand beats
160   Cold death aside and with the other sends
It back to Tybalt, whose dexterity
Retorts it. Romeo he cries aloud,
'Hold, friends! friends, part!' and swifter than his tongue,
His agile arm beats down their fatal points,
165   And 'twixt them rushes; underneath whose arm
An envious thrust from Tybalt hit the life
Of stout Mercutio, and then Tybalt fled;
But by and by comes back to Romeo,
Who had but newly entertained revenge,
170   And to't they go like lightning; for, ere I
Could draw to part them, was stout Tybalt slain;

141 *manage* course   152 *nice* trivial   155 *spleen* temper   166 *envious* ma-
licious   169 *entertained* harbored thoughts of

And, as he fell, did Romeo turn and fly.
This is the truth, or let Benvolio die.
Capulet's Wife. He is a kinsman to the Montague;
  Affection makes him false, he speaks not true.   175
  Some twenty of them fought in this black strife,
  And all those twenty could but kill one life.
  I beg for justice, which thou, Prince, must give.
  Romeo slew Tybalt; Romeo must not live.
Prince. Romeo slew him; he slew Mercutio.   180
  Who now the price of his dear blood doth owe?
Montague. Not Romeo, Prince; he was Mercutio's friend;
  His fault concludes but what the law should end,
  The life of Tybalt.
Prince.   And for that offense
  Immediately we do exile him hence.   185
  I have an interest in your hate's proceeding,
  My blood for your rude brawls doth lie a-bleeding;
  But I'll amerce you with so strong a fine
  That you shall all repent the loss of mine.
  I will be deaf to pleading and excuses;   190
  Nor tears nor prayers shall purchase out abuses.
  Therefore use none. Let Romeo hence in haste,
  Else, when he is found, that hour is his last.
  Bear hence this body, and attend our will.
  Mercy but murders, pardoning those that kill.   195

Exit, [with others].

188 *amerce* penalize   194 *attend our will* come to be judged

Enter Juliet alone.

Juliet. Gallop apace, you fiery-footed steeds,
    Towards Phoebus' lodging! Such a wagoner
    As Phaëton would whip you to the west
    And bring in cloudy night immediately.
5   Spread thy close curtain, love-performing night,
    That runaways' eyes may wink, and Romeo
    Leap to these arms untalked of and unseen.
    Lovers can see to do their amorous rites
    By their own beauties; or, if love be blind,
10   It best agrees with night. Come, civil night,
    Thou sober-suited matron, all in black,
    And learn me how to lose a winning match,
    Played for a pair of stainless maidenhoods.
    Hood my unmanned blood, bating in my cheeks,
15   With thy black mantle till strange love grow bold,
    Think true love acted simple modesty.
    Come, night; come, Romeo; come, thou day in night;
    For thou wilt lie upon the wings of night
    Whiter than new snow upon a raven's back.
20   Come, gentle night; come, loving, black-browed night;
    Give me my Romeo; and, when he shall die,
    Take him and cut him out in little stars,
    And he will make the face of heaven so fine
    That all the world will be in love with night
25   And pay no worship to the garish sun.
    O, I have bought the mansion of a love,

III, ii, 1 *steeds* horses drawing the chariot of the sun 2 *Phoebus* the sun-god *lodging* (below the western horizon) 3 *Phaëton* Phoebus' son, with whom the horses of the sun ran away 6 *runaways' eyes* eyes of the sun's horses (?) *wink* close 9 *love* Cupid 14 *Hood* cover with a hood (falconry) *unmanned* untamed *bating* fluttering 15 *strange* unfamiliar 16 *true love acted* the act of true love

But not possessed it; and though I am sold,
Not yet enjoyed. So tedious is this day
As is the night before some festival
To an impatient child that hath new robes   30
And may not wear them. O, here comes my nurse,

Enter Nurse, with cords.

And she brings news; and every tongue that speaks
But Romeo's name speaks heavenly eloquence.
Now, nurse, what news? What hast thou there, the cords
That Romeo bid thee fetch?
Nurse.   Ay, ay, the cords.   35
                              [*Throws them down.*]
Juliet. Ay me! what news? Why dost thou wring thy
    hands?
Nurse. Ah, weraday! he's dead, he's dead, he's dead!
We are undone, lady, we are undone!
Alack the day! he's gone, he's killed, he's dead!
Juliet. Can heaven be so envious?
Nurse.   Romeo can,   40
Though heaven cannot. O Romeo, Romeo!
Who ever would have thought it? Romeo!
Juliet. What devil art thou that dost torment me thus?
This torture should be roared in dismal hell.
Hath Romeo slain himself? Say thou but 'I,'   45
And that bare vowel 'I' shall poison more
Than the death-darting eye of cockatrice.
I am not I, if there be such an 'I'
Or those eyes' shot that makes the answer 'I.'

37 *weraday* welladay, alas   40 *heaven . . . envious* (cf. III, v, 211)   45–50 *I*
(with the alternate meaning 'ay')   47 *cockatrice* basilisk (a fabulous serpent
which killed with eye-glances)   49 *those eyes' shot* the Nurse's eye-glance,
which may inadvertently reveal her unspoken answer (see supplementary
note on pages 147–48)

50   If he be slain, say 'I'; or if not, 'no.'
      Brief sounds determine of my weal or woe.
      Nurse. I saw the wound, I saw it with mine eyes,
         (God save the mark!) here on his manly breast.
      A piteous corse, a bloody piteous corse;
55   Pale, pale as ashes, all bedaubed in blood,
      All in gore-blood. I swounded at the sight.
      Juliet. O, break, my heart! poor bankrout, break at once!
      To prison, eyes; ne'er look on liberty!
      Vile earth, to earth resign; end motion here,
60   And thou and Romeo press one heavy bier!
      Nurse. O Tybalt, Tybalt, the best friend I had!
      O courteous Tybalt! honest gentleman!
      That ever I should live to see thee dead!
      Juliet. What storm is this that blows so contrary?
65   Is Romeo slaught'red, and is Tybalt dead?
      My dearest cousin, and my dearer lord?
      Then, dreadful trumpet, sound the general doom!
      For who is living, if those two are gone?
      Nurse. Tybalt is gone, and Romeo banishèd;
70   Romeo that killed him, he is banishèd.
      Juliet. O God! Did Romeo's hand shed Tybalt's blood?
      Nurse. It did, it did! alas the day, it did!
      Juliet. O serpent heart, hid with a flow'ring face!
      Did ever dragon keep so fair a cave?
75   Beautiful tyrant! fiend angelical!
      Dove-feathered raven! wolvish-ravening lamb!

53 *God . . . mark* God avert the evil omen   56 *gore-blood* clotted blood
swounded swooned   57 *bankrout* bankrupt   59 *Vile earth* i.e. my body
resign return   67 *trumpet* i.e. the 'last trumpet'   *general doom* Judgment Day
72, 73 (in Q2 l. 72 is mistakenly assigned to Juliet, l. 73 to the Nurse)
73 *flow'ring face* (traditionally, the Serpent in Eden appeared to Eve with
the face of a young girl, wreathed in flowers)   75 *fiend angelical* (cf.
2 Corinthians 11:14)   76 *wolvish-ravening lamb* (cf. Matthew 7:15)

Despisèd substance of divinest show!
Just opposite to what thou justly seem'st —
A damnèd saint, an honorable villain!
O nature, what hadst thou to do in hell   80
When thou didst bower the spirit of a fiend
In mortal paradise of such sweet flesh?
Was ever book containing such vile matter
So fairly bound? O, that deceit should dwell
In such a gorgeous palace!
Nurse.   There's no trust,   85
No faith, no honesty in men; all perjured,
All forsworn, all naught, all dissemblers.
Ah, where's my man? Give me some aqua vitae.
These griefs, these woes, these sorrows make me old.
Shame come to Romeo!
Juliet.   Blistered be thy tongue   90
For such a wish! He was not born to shame.
Upon his brow shame is ashamed to sit;
For 'tis a throne where honor may be crowned
Sole monarch of the universal earth.
O, what a beast was I to chide at him!   95
Nurse. Will you speak well of him that killed your cousin?
Juliet. Shall I speak ill of him that is my husband?
Ah, poor my lord, what tongue shall smooth thy name
When I, thy three-hours wife, have mangled it?
But wherefore, villain, didst thou kill my cousin?   100
That villain cousin would have killed my husband.
Back, foolish tears, back to your native spring!
Your tributary drops belong to woe,
Which you, mistaking, offer up to joy.
My husband lives, that Tybalt would have slain;   105

81–82 *spirit . . . paradise* i.e. the Serpent in Eden 88 *aqua vitae* alcoholic
spirits 103 *tributary* tribute-paying

And Tybalt 's dead, that would have slain my husband.
All this is comfort; wherefore weep I then?
Some word there was, worser than Tybalt's death,
That murd'red me. I would forget it fain;
110 But O, it presses to my memory
Like damnèd guilty deeds to sinners' minds!
'Tybalt is dead, and Romeo – banishèd.'
That 'banishèd,' that one word 'banishèd,'
Hath slain ten thousand Tybalts. Tybalt's death
115 Was woe enough, if it had ended there;
Or, if sour woe delights in fellowship
And needly will be ranked with other griefs,
Why followèd not, when she said 'Tybalt 's dead,'
Thy father, or thy mother, nay, or both,
120 Which modern lamentation might have moved?
But with a rearward following Tybalt's death,
'Romeo is banishèd' – to speak that word
Is father, mother, Tybalt, Romeo, Juliet,
All slain, all dead. 'Romeo is banishèd' –
125 There is no end, no limit, measure, bound,
In that word's death; no words can that woe sound.
Where is my father and my mother, nurse?
Nurse. Weeping and wailing over Tybalt's corse.
Will you go to them? I will bring you thither.
Juliet. Wash they his wounds with tears? Mine shall be
130   spent,
When theirs are dry, for Romeo's banishment.
Take up those cords. Poor ropes, you are beguiled,
Both you and I, for Romeo is exiled.
He made you for a highway to my bed;
135 But I, a maid, die maiden-widowèd.

117 *needly* necessarily   120 *modern* ordinary, conventional   121 *rearward*
rearguard   128 *corse* body

Come, cords; come, nurse. I'll to my wedding bed;
And death, not Romeo, take my maidenhead!
Nurse. Hie to your chamber. I'll find Romeo
To comfort you. I wot well where he is.
Hark ye, your Romeo will be here at night.   140
I'll to him; he is hid at Laurence' cell.
Juliet. O, find him! give this ring to my true knight
And bid him come to take his last farewell.
                                        Exit [with Nurse].

                    Enter Friar [Laurence].   III, iii

Friar. Romeo, come forth; come forth, thou fearful man.
Affliction is enamored of thy parts,
And thou art wedded to calamity.

                    Enter Romeo.

Romeo. Father, what news? What is the Prince's doom?
What sorrow craves acquaintance at my hand   5
That I yet know not?
Friar.   Too familiar
Is my dear son with such sour company.
I bring thee tidings of the Prince's doom.
Romeo. What less than doomsday is the Prince's doom?
Friar. A gentler judgment vanished from his lips –   10
Not body's death, but body's banishment.
Romeo. Ha, banishment? Be merciful, say 'death';
For exile hath more terror in his look,
Much more than death. Do not say 'banishment.'

139 *wot* know   III, iii, s.d. (separate entrances in Q1; Q2 reads 'Enter
Friar and Romeo.')   1 *fearful* full of fear   2 *parts* qualities   8 *Prince's
doom* punishment decreed by the Prince   9 *doomsday* i.e. death   10 *vanished* disappeared into air

15 *Friar.* Hence from Verona art thou banishèd.
    Be patient, for the world is broad and wide.
   Romeo. There is no world without Verona walls,
    But purgatory, torture, hell itself.
    Hence banishèd is banished from the world,
20 And world's exile is death. Then 'banishèd'
    Is death mistermed. Calling death 'banishèd,'
    Thou cut'st my head off with a golden axe
    And smilest upon the stroke that murders me.
   Friar. O deadly sin! O rude unthankfulness!
25 Thy fault our law calls death; but the kind Prince,
    Taking thy part, hath rushed aside the law,
    And turned that black word 'death' to banishment.
    This is dear mercy, and thou seest it not.
   Romeo. 'Tis torture, and not mercy. Heaven is here,
30 Where Juliet lives; and every cat and dog
    And little mouse, every unworthy thing,
    Live here in heaven and may look on her;
    But Romeo may not. More validity,
    More honorable state, more courtship lives
35 In carrion flies than Romeo. They may seize
    On the white wonder of dear Juliet's hand
    And steal immortal blessing from her lips,
    Who, even in pure and vestal modesty,
    Still blush, as thinking their own kisses sin;
40 But Romeo may not, he is banishèd.
    Flies may do this but I from this must fly;
    They are freemen, but I am banishèd.
    And sayest thou yet that exile is not death?

26 *rushed* pushed   33 *validity* value   34 *courtship* privilege of wooing
38 *vestal* virgin   39 *kisses* (when her lips touch each other)   40–42 (in
Q2 these lines are preceded by 'This may flies do when I from this must
fly'—evidently a cancelled line printed in error—and by l. 43, evidently
misplaced)

Hadst thou no poison mixed, no sharp-ground knife,
No sudden mean of death, though ne'er so mean,   45
But 'banishèd' to kill me – 'banishèd'?
O friar, the damnèd use that word in hell;
Howling attends it! How hast thou the heart,
Being a divine, a ghostly confessor,
A sin-absolver, and my friend professed,   50
To mangle me with that word 'banishèd'?
Friar. Thou fond mad man, hear me a little speak.
Romeo. O, thou wilt speak again of banishment.
Friar. I'll give thee armor to keep off that word;
Adversity's sweet milk, philosophy,   55
To comfort thee, though thou art banishèd.
Romeo. Yet 'banishèd'? Hang up philosophy!
Unless philosophy can make a Juliet,
Displant a town, reverse a prince's doom,
It helps not, it prevails not. Talk no more.   60
Friar. O, then I see that madmen have no ears.
Romeo. How should they, when that wise men have no
  eyes?
Friar. Let me dispute with thee of thy estate.
Romeo. Thou canst not speak of that thou dost not feel.
Wert thou as young as I, Juliet thy love,   65
An hour but married, Tybalt murderèd,
Doting like me, and like me banishèd,
Then mightst thou speak, then mightst thou tear thy hair,
And fall upon the ground, as I do now,
Taking the measure of an unmade grave.   70
                              Enter Nurse and knock.
Friar. Arise; one knocks. Good Romeo, hide thyself.

---

45 *mean . . . mean* means . . . lowly   52 *fond* foolish   63 *dispute* reason
estate situation   70 *Taking the measure* providing the measurements   70 S.D.
(so Q2, with another entrance for Nurse at l. 78)

Romeo. Not I; unless the breath of heartsick groans
    Mist-like infold me from the search of eyes.   *[Knock.]*
Friar. Hark, how they knock! Who's there? Romeo, arise;
75   Thou wilt be taken. – Stay awhile! – Stand up; *[Knock.]*
    Run to my study. – By and by! – God's will,
    What simpleness is this. – I come, I come!   *Knock.*
    Who knocks so hard? Whence come you? What's your
       will?

Enter Nurse.

Nurse. Let me come in, and you shall know my errand.
    I come from Lady Juliet.
80 *Friar.*   Welcome then.
Nurse. O holy friar, O, tell me, holy friar,
    Where is my lady's lord, where's Romeo?
Friar. There on the ground, with his own tears made
    drunk.
Nurse. O, he is even in my mistress' case,
85   Just in her case! O woeful sympathy!
    Piteous predicament! Even so lies she,
    Blubb'ring and weeping, weeping and blubb'ring.
    Stand up, stand up! Stand, an you be a man.
    For Juliet's sake, for her sake, rise and stand!
90   Why should you fall into so deep an O?
Romeo. [rises] Nurse –
Nurse. Ah sir! ah sir! Death's the end of all.
Romeo. Spakest thou of Juliet? How is it with her?
    Doth not she think me an old murderer,
95   Now I have stained the childhood of our joy
    With blood removed but little from her own?

73 S.D. (Q2 reads 'They knock.') 75 S.D. (Q2 reads 'Slud knock.') 76 *By
and by* in a moment 77 *simpleness* stupid conduct 90 *an O* a fit of groaning
94 *old* hardened

Where is she? and how doth she! and what says
My concealed lady to our cancelled love?
Nurse. O, she says nothing, sir, but weeps and weeps;
And now falls on her bed, and then starts up,   100
And Tybalt calls; and then on Romeo cries,
And then down falls again.
Romeo.   As if that name,
Shot from the deadly level of a gun,
Did murder her; as that name's cursèd hand
Murdered her kinsman. O, tell me, friar, tell me,   105
In what vile part of this anatomy
Doth my name lodge? Tell me, that I may sack
The hateful mansion.
[He offers to stab himself, and Nurse snatches the dagger away.]
Friar.   Hold thy desperate hand.
Art thou a man? Thy form cries out thou art;
Thy tears are womanish, thy wild acts denote   110
The unreasonable fury of a beast.
Unseemly woman in a seeming man!
And ill-beseeming beast in seeming both!
Thou hast amazed me. By my holy order,
I thought thy disposition better tempered.   115
Hast thou slain Tybalt? Wilt thou slay thyself?
And slay thy lady that in thy life lives,
By doing damnèd hate upon thyself?
Why railest thou on thy birth, the heaven, and earth?
Since birth and heaven and earth, all three do meet   120

98 *concealed . . . cancelled* hidden from me . . . invalidated by my act (the
two words were given almost the same pronunciation) 103 *level* aim
106 *anatomy* body 108 S.D. (from Q1) 111 *unreasonable* irrational 112
Unseemly . . . seeming disorderly . . . apparent 113 *ill-beseeming . . . both*
inappropriate . . . man and woman 117 *in . . . lives* (cf. II, i, 1 and note)
120 *all . . . meet* the soul comes from heaven, the body from earth; they
unite in man at his birth

In thee at once; which thou at once wouldst lose.
Fie, fie, thou shamest thy shape, thy love, thy wit,
Which, like a usurer, abound'st in all,
And usest none in that true use indeed
125 Which should bedeck thy shape, thy love, thy wit.
Thy noble shape is but a form of wax,
Digressing from the valor of a man;
Thy dear love sworn but hollow perjury,
Killing that love which thou hast vowed to cherish;
130 Thy wit, that ornament to shape and love,
Misshapen in the conduct of them both,
Like powder in a skilless soldier's flask,
Is set afire by thine own ignorance,
And thou dismemb'red with thine own defense.
135 What, rouse thee, man! Thy Juliet is alive,
For whose dear sake thou wast but lately dead.
There art thou happy. Tybalt would kill thee,
But thou slewest Tybalt. There art thou happy too.
The law, that threat'ned death, becomes thy friend
140 And turns it to exile. There art thou happy.
A pack of blessings light upon thy back;
Happiness courts thee in her best array;
But, like a misbehaved and sullen wench,
Thou pout'st upon thy fortune and thy love.
145 Take heed, take heed, for such die miserable.
Go get thee to thy love, as was decreed,
Ascend her chamber, hence and comfort her.
But look thou stay not till the watch be set,
For then thou canst not pass to Mantua,

123 *Which* (you) who *all* all capabilities 124 *true use* proper handling
of wealth 126 *form of wax* waxwork, outward appearance 129 *Killing*
that love (cf. l. 117) 130 *wit* intellect 131 *Misshapen* distorted *conduct*
guidance 132 *flask* powder horn 134 *defense* i.e. intellect 136 *dead* as
one dead 137 *happy* fortunate

Where thou shalt live till we can find a time   150
To blaze your marriage, reconcile your friends,
Beg pardon of the Prince, and call thee back
With twenty hundred thousand times more joy
Than thou went'st forth in lamentation.
Go before, nurse. Commend me to thy lady,   155
And bid her hasten all the house to bed,
Which heavy sorrow makes them apt unto.
Romeo is coming.
Nurse. O Lord, I could have stayed here all the night
To hear good counsel. O, what learning is!   160
My lord, I'll tell my lady you will come.
Romeo. Do so, and bid my sweet prepare to chide.
Nurse. Here is a ring she bid me give you, sir.
Hie you, make haste, for it grows very late.   *[Exit.]*
Romeo. How well my comfort is revived by this!   165
Friar. Go hence; good night; and here stands all your state:
Either be gone before the watch be set,
Or by the break of day disguised from hence.
Sojourn in Mantua. I'll find out your man,
And he shall signify from time to time   170
Every good hap to you that chances here.
Give me thy hand. 'Tis late. Farewell; good night.
Romeo. But that a joy past joy calls out on me,
It were a grief so brief to part with thee.
Farewell.   *Exeunt.* 175

151 *blaze* publish   166 *here . . . state* here is your situation

III, iv   *Enter old Capulet, his Wife, and Paris.*

Capulet. Things have fall'n out, sir, so unluckily
      That we have had no time to move our daughter.
      Look you, she loved her kinsman Tybalt dearly,
      And so did I. Well, we were born to die.
5   'Tis very late; she'll not come down to-night.
      I promise you, but for your company,
      I would have been abed an hour ago.
Paris. These times of woe afford no times to woo.
      Madam, good night. Commend me to your daughter.
10 *Lady.* I will, and know her mind early to-morrow;
      To-night she's mewed up to her heaviness.
Capulet. Sir Paris, I will make a desperate tender
      Of my child's love. I think she will be ruled
      In all respects by me; nay more, I doubt it not.
15   Wife, go you to her ere you go to bed;
      Acquaint her here of my son Paris' love
      And bid her (mark you me?) on Wednesday next —
      But soft! what day is this?
Paris.   Monday, my lord.
Capulet. Monday! ha, ha! Well, Wednesday is too soon.
20   A Thursday let it be — a Thursday, tell her,
      She shall be married to this noble earl.
      Will you be ready? Do you like this haste?
      We'll keep no great ado — a friend or two;
      For hark you, Tybalt being slain so late,
25   It may be thought we held him carelessly,
      Being our kinsman, if we revel much.
      Therefore we'll have some half a dozen friends,
      And there an end. But what say you to Thursday?

III, iv, 2 *move* talk with   11 *mewed up* shut up (falconry)   *heaviness* grief
12 *desperate tender* risk-taking offer   20 *A* on

Paris. My lord, I would that Thursday were to-morrow.
Capulet. Well, get you gone. A Thursday be it then.   30
  Go you to Juliet ere you go to bed;
  Prepare her, wife, against this wedding day.
  Farewell, my lord. — Light to my chamber, ho!,
  Afore me, it is so very very late
  That we may call it early by and by.   35
  Good night.   *Exeunt.*

❈

   Enter Romeo and Juliet aloft, [at the window].   III, v

Juliet. Wilt thou be gone? It is not yet near day.
  It was the nightingale, and not the lark,
  That pierced the fearful hollow of thine ear.
  Nightly she sings on yond pomegranate tree.
  Believe me, love, it was the nightingale.   5
Romeo. It was the lark, the herald of the morn;
  No nightingale. Look, love, what envious streaks
  Do lace the severing clouds in yonder East.
  Night's candles are burnt out, and jocund day
  Stands tiptoe on the misty mountain tops.   10
  I must be gone and live, or stay and die.
Juliet. Yond light is not daylight; I know it, I.
  It is some meteor that the sun exhales
  To be to thee this night a torchbearer
  And light thee on thy way to Mantua.   15
  Therefore stay yet; thou need'st not to be gone.
Romeo. Let me be ta'en, let me be put to death.

34 *Afore me* (a light oath) 35 *by and by* immediately III, v, s.d. *at the
window* (from Q1) 3 *fearful* apprehensive 9 *Night's candles* the stars
13 *meteor* nocturnal light, such as the will-o'-the-wisp, supposedly of
luminous gas given off by the sun or drawn by his power (*exhaled*) out
of marshy ground

I am content, so thou wilt have it so.
I'll say yon grey is not the morning's eye,
20 'Tis but the pale reflex of Cynthia's brow;
Nor that is not the lark whose notes do beat
The vaulty heaven so high above our heads.
I have more care to stay than will to go.
Come, death, and welcome! Juliet wills it so.
25 How is't, my soul? Let's talk; it is not day.
   Juliet. It is, it is! Hie hence, be gone, away!
It is the lark that sings so out of tune,
Straining harsh discords and unpleasing sharps.
Some say the lark makes sweet division;
30 This doth not so, for she divideth us.
Some say the lark and loathèd toad change eyes;
O, now I would they had changed voices too,
Since arm from arm that voice doth us affray,
Hunting thee hence with hunt's-up to the day.
35 O, now be gone! More light and light it grows.
   Romeo. More light and light – more dark and dark our
    woes.

Enter Nurse [hastily].

Nurse. Madam!
Juliet. Nurse?
Nurse. Your lady mother is coming to your chamber.
40 The day is broke; be wary, look about.   *[Exit.]*
Juliet. Then, window, let day in, and let life out.
Romeo. Farewell, farewell! One kiss, and I'll descend.
                       [He goeth down.]

20 *reflex . . . brow* reflection of the moon   25 *my soul* (cf. II, ii, 165)
29 *division* melody   31 *change* exchange (a folk belief)   33 *affray* frighten
34 *hunt's-up* morning song to awaken huntsmen   36 s.d. *hastily* (from Q1;
Q2 reads 'Enter Madam and Nurse.')   41 *life* (cf. III, iii, 117)   42 s.d.
(from Q1)

Juliet. Art thou gone so, love-lord, ay husband-friend?
  I must hear from thee every day in the hour,
  For in a minute there are many days.   45
  O, by this count I shall be much in years
  Ere I again behold my Romeo!
Romeo. Farewell!
  I will omit no opportunity
  That may convey my greetings, love, to thee.   50
Juliet. O, think'st thou we shall ever meet again?
Romeo. I doubt it not; and all these woes shall serve
  For sweet discourses in our times to come.
Juliet. O God, I have an ill-divining soul!
  Methinks I see thee, now thou art so low,   55
  As one dead in the bottom of a tomb.
  Either my eyesight fails, or thou lookest pale.
Romeo. And trust me, love, in my eye so do you.
  Dry sorrow drinks our blood. Adieu, adieu!   *Exit.*
Juliet. O Fortune, Fortune! all men call thee fickle.   60
  If thou art fickle, what dost thou with him
  That is renowned for faith? Be fickle, Fortune,
  For then I hope thou wilt not keep him long
  But send him back.   [*She goeth down from the window.*]

Enter Mother.

Lady. Ho, daughter! are you up?   65
Juliet. Who is't that calls? It is my lady mother.
  Is she not down so late, or up so early?
  What unaccustomed cause procures her hither?

43 *friend* clandestine lover   46 *much* advanced   54 *ill-divining* prophetic
of evil   59 *Dry . . . blood* (the presumed effect of grief was to dry up the
blood)   64 s.d. (from Q1, and so placed that it might apply only to
the Nurse; but since the Q1 stage direction immediately following is
'Enter Juliet's Mother, Nurse,' the indications are that the subsequent
action takes place below, where Juliet joins her mother)   67 *down* abed

Lady. Why, how now, Juliet?

Juliet.   Madam, I am not well.

70 *Lady.* Evermore weeping for your cousin's death?
What, wilt thou wash him from his grave with tears?
An if thou couldst, thou couldst not make him live.
Therefore have done. Some grief shows much of love;
But much of grief shows still some want of wit.

75 *Juliet.* Yet let me weep for such a feeling loss.

Lady. So shall you feel the loss, but not the friend
Which you weep for.

Juliet.   Feeling so the loss,
I cannot choose but ever weep the friend.

Lady. Well, girl, thou weep'st not so much for his death
80 As that the villain lives which slaughtered him.

Juliet. What villain, madam?

Lady.   That same villain Romeo.

Juliet. [*aside*] Villain and he be many miles asunder. —
God pardon him! I do, with all my heart;
And yet no man like he doth grieve my heart.

85 *Lady.* That is because the traitor murderer lives.

Juliet. Ay, madam, from the reach of these my hands.
Would none but I might venge my cousin's death!

Lady. We will have vengeance for it, fear thou not.
Then weep no more. I'll send to one in Mantua,
90 Where that same banished runagate doth live,
Shall give him such an unaccustomed dram
That he shall soon keep Tybalt company;
And then I hope thou wilt be satisfied.

Juliet. Indeed I never shall be satisfied
95 With Romeo till I behold him — dead —
Is my poor heart so for a kinsman vexed.

75 *feeling* deeply felt   84 *like* so much as   90 *runagate* renegade

108

Madam, if you could find out but a man
To bear a poison, I would temper it;
That Romeo should, upon receipt thereof,
Soon sleep in quiet. O, how my heart abhors   100
To hear him named and cannot come to him,
To wreak the love I bore my cousin
Upon his body that hath slaughtered him!
Lady. Find thou the means, and I'll find such a man.
But now I'll tell thee joyful tidings, girl.   105
Juliet. And joy comes well in such a needy time.
What are they, beseech your ladyship?
Lady. Well, well, thou hast a careful father, child;
One who, to put thee from thy heaviness,
Hath sorted out a sudden day of joy   110
That thou expects not nor I looked not for.
Juliet. Madam, in happy time! What day is that?
Lady. Marry, my child, early next Thursday morn
The gallant, young, and noble gentleman,
The County Paris, at Saint Peter's Church,   115
Shall happily make thee there a joyful bride.
Juliet. Now by Saint Peter's Church, and Peter too,
He shall not make me there a joyful bride!
I wonder at this haste, that I must wed
Ere he that should be husband comes to woo.   120
I pray you tell my lord and father, madam,
I will not marry yet; and when I do, I swear
It shall be Romeo, whom you know I hate,
Rather than Paris. These are news indeed!
Lady. Here comes your father. Tell him so yourself, 125
And see how he will take it at your hands.

98 *temper* prepare or concoct (with play on 'moderate')   110 *sorted* chosen
112 *in happy time* opportunely

Enter Capulet and Nurse.

Capulet. When the sun sets the earth doth drizzle dew,
    But for the sunset of my brother's son
    It rains downright.
130   How now? a conduit, girl? What, still in tears?
    Evermore show'ring? In one little body
    Thou counterfeit'st a bark, a sea, a wind:
    For still thy eyes, which I may call the sea,
    Do ebb and flow with tears; the bark thy body is,
135   Sailing in this salt flood; the winds, thy sighs,
    Who, raging with thy tears and they with them,
    Without a sudden calm will overset
    Thy tempest-tossèd body. How now, wife?
    Have you deliverèd to her our decree?
140 *Lady.* Ay, sir; but she will none, she gives you thanks.
    I would the fool were married to her grave!
Capulet. Soft! take me with you, take me with you,
    wife.
    How? Will she none? Doth she not give us thanks?
    Is she not proud? Doth she not count her blest,
145   Unworthy as she is, that we have wrought
    So worthy a gentleman to be her bride?
Juliet. Not proud you have, but thankful that you have.
    Proud can I never be of what I hate,
    But thankful even for hate that is meant love.
Capulet. How, how, how, how, chopped-logic? What is
150   this?
    'Proud' — and 'I thank you' — and 'I thank you not' —
    And yet 'not proud'? Mistress minion you,

130 *conduit* water-pipe   137 *sudden* immediate   140 *gives you thanks* says
'No, thank you'   141 *married . . . grave* (a petulant but prophetic comment,
like l. 167 below)   142 *take . . . you* let me understand you   145 *wrought*
arranged for   146 *bride* bridegroom   150 *chopped-logic* hair-splitting

Thank me no thankings, nor proud me no prouds,
But fettle your fine joints 'gainst Thursday next
To go with Paris to Saint Peter's Church,   155
Or I will drag thee on a hurdle thither.
Out, you green-sickness carrion! out, you baggage!
You tallow-face!
Lady.   Fie, fie! what, are you mad?
Juliet. Good father, I beseech you on my knees,
Hear me with patience but to speak a word.   160
Capulet. Hang thee, young baggage! disobedient wretch!
I tell thee what — get thee to church a Thursday
Or never after look me in the face.
Speak not, reply not, do not answer me!
My fingers itch. Wife, we scarce thought us blest   165
That God had lent us but this only child;
But now I see this one is one too much,
And that we have a curse in having her.
Out on her, hilding!
Nurse.   God in heaven bless her!
You are to blame, my lord, to rate her so.   170
Capulet. And why, my Lady Wisdom? Hold your tongue,
Good Prudence. Smatter with your gossips, go!
Nurse. I speak no treason.
Capulet.   O, God-i-god-en!
Nurse. May not one speak?
Capulet.   Peace, you mumbling fool!
Utter your gravity o'er a gossip's bowl,   175
For here we need it not.
Lady.   You are too hot.

---

154 *fettle* prepare 156 *hurdle* sledge on which criminals were carried to
execution 157 *green-sickness* anaemic *baggage* worthless woman 158
tallow-face pale-face *are you mad* (addressed to Capulet) 162 *a* on 169
hilding worthless creature 170 *rate* scold 172 *Smatter . . . gossips* chatter
with your cronies 173 *God-i-god-en* for God's sake

Capulet. God's bread! it makes me mad.

 Day, night; hour, tide, time; work, play;

 Alone, in company; still my care hath been

180 To have her matched; and having now provided

 A gentleman of noble parentage,

 Of fair demesnes, youthful, and nobly trained,

 Stuffed, as they say, with honorable parts,

 Proportioned as one's thought would wish a man —

185 And then to have a wretched puling fool,

 A whining mammet, in her fortune's tender,

 To answer 'I'll not wed, I cannot love;

 I am too young, I pray you pardon me'!

 But, an you will not wed, I'll pardon you!

190 Graze where you will, you shall not house with me.

 Look to't, think on't; I do not use to jest.

 Thursday is near; lay hand on heart, advise:

 An you be mine, I'll give you to my friend;

 An you be not, hang, beg, starve, die in the streets,

195 For, by my soul, I'll ne'er acknowledge thee,

 Nor what is mine shall never do thee good.

 Trust to't. Bethink you. I'll not be forsworn.   *Exit.*

Juliet. Is there no pity sitting in the clouds

 That sees into the bottom of my grief?

200 O sweet my mother, cast me not away!

 Delay this marriage for a month, a week;

 Or if you do not, make the bridal bed

 In that dim monument where Tybalt lies.

---

177 *bread* bread of the Sacrament   178-79 *Day . . . company* (in Q1 the
equivalent matter occupies two separate lines: 'Day, night; early, late; at
home, abroad; Alone, in company; waking or sleeping;'—more logical,
but irreconcilable with the Q2 passage except by guesswork)   182 *demesnes* domains   185 *puling* whining   186 *mammet* doll   *tender* offer
189 *I'll pardon you* (ironic)   191 *do not use* am not accustomed   192 *advise*
consider

Lady. Talk not to me, for I'll not speak a word.
 Do as thou wilt, for I have done with thee.   *Exit.* 205
Juliet. O God! — O nurse, how shall this be prevented?
 My husband is on earth, my faith in heaven.
 How shall that faith return again to earth
 Unless that husband send it me from heaven
 By leaving earth? Comfort me, counsel me.   210
 Alack, alack, that heaven should practise stratagems
 Upon so soft a subject as myself!
 What say'st thou? Hast thou not a word of joy?
 Some comfort, nurse.
Nurse.   Faith, here it is
 Romeo is banished; and all the world to nothing   215
 That he dares ne'er come back to challenge you;
 Or if he do, it needs must be by stealth.
 Then, since the case so stands as now it doth,
 I think it best you married with the County.
 O, he's a lovely gentleman!   220
 Romeo's a dishclout to him. An eagle, madam,
 Hath not so green, so quick, so fair an eye
 As Paris hath. Beshrew my very heart,
 I think you are happy in this second match,
 For it excels your first; or if it did not,   225
 Your first is dead — or 'twere as good he were
 As living here and you no use of him.
Juliet. Speak'st thou from thy heart?
Nurse. And from my soul too; else beshrew them both.
Juliet. Amen!   230
Nurse. What?

207 *my faith in heaven* my marriage vow is recorded in heaven 208–10
How . . . earth how can I marry unless I am first widowed 215 *all . . .
nothing* i.e. it is a safe bet 216 *challenge* demand possession of 221 *dishclout*
dishcloth 229 *beshrew* a curse on

113

Juliet. Well, thou hast comforted me marvellous much.
    Go in; and tell my lady I am gone,
    Having displeased my father, to Laurence' cell,
235 To make confession and to be absolved.
Nurse. Marry, I will; and this is wisely done.   *[Exit.]*
Juliet. Ancient damnation! O most wicked fiend!
    Is it more sin to wish me thus forsworn,
    Or to dispraise my lord with that same tongue
240 Which she hath praised him with above compare
    So many thousand times? Go, counsellor!
    Thou and my bosom henceforth shall be twain.
    I'll to the friar to know his remedy.
    If all else fail, myself have power to die.   *Exit.*

❈

IV, i   *Enter Friar [Laurence] and County Paris.*

Friar. On Thursday, sir? The time is very short.
Paris. My father Capulet will have it so,
    And I am nothing slow to slack his haste.
Friar. You say you do not know the lady's mind.
5   Uneven is the course; I like it not.
Paris. Immoderately she weeps for Tybalt's death,
    And therefore have I little talked of love;
    For Venus smiles not in a house of tears.
    Now, sir, her father counts it dangerous
10 That she do give her sorrow so much sway,
    And in his wisdom hastes our marriage

237 *Ancient damnation* damnable old woman   242 *bosom* confidence
twain separated   IV, i, 5 *course* i.e. race course   8 *Venus . . . tears* the
influence of the planet Venus is unfavorable when she appears in the
'house' of a 'moist' constellation, such as Pisces or Aquarius; i.e. one
cannot talk of love amidst grief

To stop the inundation of her tears,
Which, too much minded by herself alone,
May be put from her by society.
Now do you know the reason of this haste.   15
Friar. [*aside*] I would I knew not why it should be slowed. —
Look, sir, here comes the lady toward my cell.

Enter Juliet.

Paris. Happily met, my lady and my wife!
Juliet. That may be, sir, when I may be a wife.
Paris. That 'may be' must be, love, on Thursday next.   20
Juliet. What must be shall be.
Friar.   That's a certain text.
Paris. Come you to make confession to this father?
Juliet. To answer that, I should confess to you.
Paris. Do not deny to him that you love me.
Juliet. I will confess to you that I love him.   25
Paris. So will ye, I am sure, that you love me.
Juliet. If I do so, it will be of more price,
     Being spoke behind your back, than to your face.
Paris. Poor soul, thy face is much abused with tears.
Juliet. The tears have got small victory by that,   30
     For it was bad enough before their spite.
Paris. Thou wrong'st it more than tears with that report.
Juliet. That is no slander, sir, which is a truth;
     And what I spake, I spake it to my face.
Paris. Thy face is mine, and thou hast sland'red it.   35
Juliet. It may be so, for it is not mine own.
     Are you at leisure, holy father, now,
     Or shall I come to you at evening mass?
Friar. My leisure serves me, pensive daughter, now.
     My lord, we must entreat the time alone.   40

13 *minded* thought about

115

Paris. God shield I should disturb devotion!
    Juliet, on Thursday early will I rouse ye.
    Till then, adieu, and keep this holy kiss.   *Exit.*
Juliet. O, shut the door! and when thou hast done so,
45   Come weep with me — past hope, past cure, past help!
Friar. Ah, Juliet, I already know thy grief;
    It strains me past the compass of my wits.
    I hear thou must, and nothing may prorogue it,
    On Thursday next be married to this County.
50 *Juliet.* Tell me not, friar, that thou hearest of this,
    Unless thou tell me how I may prevent it.
    If in thy wisdom thou canst give no help,
    Do thou but call my resolution wise
    And with this knife I'll help it presently.
55   God joined my heart and Romeo's, thou our hands;
    And ere this hand, by thee to Romeo's sealed,
    Shall be the label to another deed,
    Or my true heart with treacherous revolt
    Turn to another, this shall slay them both.
60   Therefore, out of thy long-experienced time,
    Give me some present counsel; or, behold,
    'Twixt my extremes and me this bloody knife
    Shall play the umpire, arbitrating that
    Which the commission of thy years and art
65   Could to no issue of true honor bring.
    Be not so long to speak. I long to die
    If what thou speak'st speak not of remedy.
Friar. Hold, daughter. I do spy a kind of hope,
    Which craves as desperate an execution

41 *shield* forbid 47 *the compass . . . wits* my wits' end 48 *prorogue* postpone 57 *label* i.e. strip of parchment bearing the seal, attached to a deed 60 *time* age 62 *extremes* difficulties 64 *commission . . . art* authority of your age and skill

As that is desperate which we would prevent.   70
If, rather than to marry County Paris,
Thou hast the strength of will to slay thyself,
Then is it likely thou wilt undertake
A thing like death to chide away this shame,
That cop'st with death himself to scape from it;   75
And, if thou darest, I'll give thee remedy.
Juliet. O, bid me leap, rather than marry Paris,
From off the battlements of any tower,
Or walk in thievish ways, or bid me lurk
Where serpents are; chain me with roaring bears,   80
Or hide me nightly in a charnel house,
O'ercovered quite with dead men's rattling bones,
With reeky shanks and yellow chapless skulls;
Or bid me go into a new-made grave
And hide me with a dead man in his shroud —   85
Things that, to hear them told, have made me tremble —
And I will do it without fear or doubt,
To live an unstained wife to my sweet love.
Friar. Hold, then. Go home, be merry, give consent
To marry Paris. Wednesday is to-morrow.   90
To-morrow night look that thou lie alone;
Let not the nurse lie with thee in thy chamber.
Take thou this vial, being then in bed,
And this distilling liquor drink thou off;
When presently through all thy veins shall run   95
A cold and drowsy humor; for no pulse
Shall keep his native progress, but surcease;
No warmth, no breath, shall testify thou livest;
The roses in thy lips and cheeks shall fade

75 *cop'st* encounterest 79 *thievish ways* roads frequented by robbers
81 *charnel house* depository of human bones 83 *reeky* smelly *chapless*
jawless 94 *distilling* infusing 96 *humor* moisture 97 *surcease* cease

100   To wanny ashes, thy eyes' windows fall
      Like death when he shuts up the day of life;
      Each part, deprived of supple government,
      Shall, stiff and stark and cold, appear like death;
      And in this borrowèd likeness of shrunk death
105   Thou shalt continue two-and-forty hours,
      And then awake as from a pleasant sleep.
      Now, when the bridegroom in the morning comes
      To rouse thee from thy bed, there art thou dead.
      Then, as the manner of our country is,
110   In thy best robes uncoverèd on the bier
      Thou shalt be borne to that same ancient vault
      Where all the kindred of the Capulets lie.
      In the mean time, against thou shalt awake,
      Shall Romeo by my letters know our drift;
115   And hither shall he come; and he and I
      Will watch thy waking, and that very night
      Shall Romeo bear thee hence to Mantua.
      And this shall free thee from this present shame,
      If no inconstant toy nor womanish fear
120   Abate thy valor in the acting it.
   Juliet. Give me, give me! O, tell not me of fear!
   Friar. Hold! Get you gone, be strong and prosperous
      In this resolve. I'll send a friar with speed
      To Mantua, with my letters to thy lord.
125 *Juliet.* Love give me strength! and strength shall help afford.
      Farewell, dear father.   *Exit [with Friar].*

❊

100 *wanny* pale, shrunken *windows* i.e. eyelids (the figure derives from the covering of shop-fronts at the close of the day) 102 *supple government* the life force that keeps the body supple 111 (in Q2 this line is preceded by 'Be borne to burial in thy kindred's grave,' evidently a cancelled version of the line, printed in error) 113 *against . . . awake* in preparation for your awaking 114 *drift* intention 119 *toy* whim

Enter Father Capulet, Mother, Nurse, and Servingmen,   IV, ii
  two or three.

Capulet. So many guests invite as here are writ.
                                    [Exit a Servingman.]
  Sirrah, go hire me twenty cunning cooks.
Servingman. You shall have none ill, sir; for I'll try if they
  can lick their fingers.
Capulet. How canst thou try them so?   5
Servingman. Marry, sir, 'tis an ill cook that cannot lick his
  own fingers. Therefore he that cannot lick his fingers
  goes not with me.
Capulet. Go, begone.   *[Exit Servingman.]*
  We shall be much unfurnished for this time.   10
  What, is my daughter gone to Friar Laurence?
Nurse. Ay, forsooth.
Capulet. Well, he may chance to do some good on her.
  A peevish self-willed harlotry it is.

Enter Juliet.

Nurse. See where she comes from shrift with merry look. 15
Capulet. How now, my headstrong? Where have you been
  gadding?
Juliet. Where I have learnt me to repent the sin
  Of disobedient opposition
  To you and your behests, and am enjoined
  By holy Laurence to fall prostrate here   20
  To beg your pardon. Pardon, I beseech you!
  Henceforward I am ever ruled by you.

IV, ii, 5 *try* test 6–7 *'tis . . . fingers* it's a poor cook who doesn't like to
taste the food which he prepares (proverbial) 10 *unfurnished* unprovided
14 *harlotry* hussy

Capulet. Send for the County. Go tell him of this.
    I'll have this knot knit up to-morrow morning.
25 *Juliet.* I met the youthful lord at Laurence' cell
    And gave him what becomèd love I might,
    Not stepping o'er the bounds of modesty.
Capulet. Why, I am glad on't. This is well. Stand up.
    This is as't should be. Let me see the County.
30 Ay, marry, go, I say, and fetch him hither.
    Now, afore God, this reverend holy friar,
    All our whole city is much bound to him.
Juliet. Nurse, will you go with me into my closet
    To help me sort such needful ornaments
35 As you think fit to furnish me to-morrow?
Mother. No, not till Thursday. There is time enough.
Capulet. Go, nurse, go with her. We'll to church to-
    morrow.   *Exeunt [Juliet and Nurse].*
Mother. We shall be short in our provision.
    'Tis now near night.
Capulet.   Tush, I will stir about,
40 And all things shall be well, I warrant thee, wife.
    Go thou to Juliet, help to deck up her.
    I'll not to bed to-night; let me alone.
    I'll play the housewife for this once. What, ho!
    They are all forth; well, I will walk myself
45 To County Paris, to prepare up him
    Against to-morrow. My heart is wondrous light,
    Since this same wayward girl is so reclaimed.
                       Exit [with Mother].

24 *to-morrow morning* (i.e. Wednesday, one day earlier than planned) 32
bound indebted

Enter Juliet and Nurse.

Juliet. Ay, those attires are best; but, gentle nurse,
  I pray thee leave me to myself to-night;
  For I have need of many orisons
  To move the heavens to smile upon my state,
  Which, well thou knowest, is cross and full of sin.   5

Enter Mother.

Mother. What, are you busy, ho? Need you my help?
Juliet. No, madam; we have culled such necessaries
  As are behoveful for our state to-morrow.
  So please you, let me now be left alone,
  And let the nurse this night sit up with you;   10
  For I am sure you have your hands full all
  In this so sudden business.
Mother.   Good night.
  Get thee to bed, and rest; for thou hast need.
                    Exeunt [Mother and Nurse].
Juliet. Farewell! God knows when we shall meet again.
  I have a faint cold fear thrills through my veins   15
  That almost freezes up the heat of life.
  I'll call them back again to comfort me.
  Nurse! – What should she do here?
  My dismal scene I needs must act alone.
  Come, vial.   20
  What if this mixture do not work at all?
  Shall I be married then to-morrow morning?
  No, no! This shall forbid it. Lie thou there.
                    [Lays down a dagger.]
  What if it be a poison which the friar

IV, iii, 3 *orisons* prayers 5 *cross* perverse 7 *culled* picked out 8 *behoveful*
fitting *state* ceremony 15 *faint* causing faintness

25   Subtly hath minist'red to have me dead,
      Lest in this marriage he should be dishonored
      Because he married me before to Romeo?
      I fear it is; and yet methinks it should not,
      For he hath still been tried a holy man.
30   How if, when I am laid into the tomb,
      I wake before the time that Romeo
      Come to redeem me? There's a fearful point!
      Shall I not then be stifled in the vault,
      To whose foul mouth no healthsome air breathes in,
35   And there die strangled ere my Romeo comes?
      Or, if I live, is it not very like
      The horrible conceit of death and night,
      Together with the terror of the place —
      As in a vault, an ancient receptacle
40   Where for this many hundred years the bones
      Of all my buried ancestors are packed;
      Where bloody Tybalt, yet but green in earth,
      Lies fest'ring in his shroud; where, as they say,
      At some hours in the night spirits resort —
45   Alack, alack, is it not like that I,
      So early waking — what with loathsome smells,
      And shrieks like mandrakes torn out of the earth,
      That living mortals, hearing them, run mad —
      O, if I wake, shall I not be distraught,
50   Environèd with all these hideous fears,
      And madly play with my forefathers' joints,
      And pluck the mangled Tybalt from his shroud,
      And, in this rage, with some great kinsman's bone

25 *minist'red* administered   29 *tried* proved (after this line, Q1 inserts 'I will not entertain so bad a thought')   37 *conceit* imagination   42 *green* new   45 *like* likely   47 *mandrakes* mandragora (a narcotic plant with a forked root resembling the human form, supposed to utter maddening shrieks when uprooted)

As with a club dash out my desp'rate brains?
O, look! methinks I see my cousin's ghost   55
Seeking out Romeo, that did spit his body
Upon a rapier's point. Stay, Tybalt, stay!
Romeo, I come! this do I drink to thee.
                    [She falls upon her bed within the curtains.]

❧

Enter Lady of the House and Nurse.   IV, iv

Lady. Hold, take these keys and fetch more spices, nurse.
Nurse. They call for dates and quinces in the pastry.

Enter old Capulet.

Capulet. Come, stir, stir, stir! The second cock hath crowed,
    The curfew bell hath rung, 'tis three o'clock.
    Look to the baked meats, good Angelica;   5
    Spare not for cost.
Nurse.   Go, you cot-quean, go,
    Get you to bed! Faith, you'll be sick to-morrow
    For this night's watching.
Capulet. No, not a whit. What, I have watched ere now
    All night for lesser cause, and ne'er been sick.   10
Lady. Ay, you have been a mouse-hunt in your time;
    But I will watch you from such watching now.
                            Exit Lady and Nurse.
Capulet. A jealous hood, a jealous hood!

58 S.D. (from Q1)   IV, iv, 5 *baked meats* meat pies   6 *cot-quean* a man
who plays housewife   8 *watching* staying awake   11 *mouse-hunt* i.e. a
nocturnal prowler after women   13 *A jealous hood* you wear the cap (or
hood) of jealousy

*Enter three or four [Fellows] with spits and logs and
 baskets.*

            Now, fellow,
 What is there?

15 *1. Fellow.* Things for the cook, sir; but I know not what.
  Capulet. Make haste, make haste. *[Exit first Fellow.]* Sirrah,
   fetch drier logs.
  Call Peter; he will show thee where they are.
  2. Fellow. I have a head, sir, that will find out logs
  And never trouble Peter for the matter.

20 *Capulet.* Mass, and well said; a merry whoreson, ha!
  Thou shalt be loggerhead. *[Exit second Fellow, with the
   others.]* Good Father! 'tis day.
  The County will be here with music straight,
  For so he said he would.   *Play music.*
       I hear him near.
  Nurse! Wife! What, ho! What, nurse, I say!

Enter Nurse.

25 Go waken Juliet; go and trim her up.
  I'll go and chat with Paris. Hie, make haste,
  Make haste! The bridegroom he is come already:
  Make haste, I say.   *[Exit.]*

IV, v   *[Nurse goes to curtains.]*

Nurse. Mistress! what, mistress! Juliet! Fast, I warrant her,
  she.
 Why, lamb! why, lady! Fie, you slug-abed.
 Why, love, I say! madam! sweetheart! Why, bride!

15, 18 *1. Fellow, 2. Fellow* (Q2 reads 'Fellow' in both instances) 18 *I . . .
logs* i.e. my head is wooden and has an affinity for logs 20 *Mass* by the
Mass *whoreson* bastard, rascal 21 *loggerhead* blockhead 25 *trim her up*
dress her neatly IV, v, 1 *Fast* fast asleep 2 *slug-abed* sleepyhead

What, not a word? You take your pennyworths now;
Sleep for a week; for the next night, I warrant,   5
The County Paris hath set up his rest
That you shall rest but little. God forgive me!
Marry, and amen. How sound is she asleep!
I needs must wake her. Madam, madam, madam!
Ay, let the County take you in your bed;   10
He'll fright you up, i' faith. Will it not be?
                              [Draws aside the curtains.]
What, dressed, and in your clothes, and down again?
I must needs wake you. Lady! lady! lady!
Alas, alas! Help, help! my lady 's dead!
O weraday that ever I was born!   15
Some aqua vitae, ho! My lord! my lady!

[Enter Mother.]

Mother. What noise is here?
Nurse.   O lamentable day!
Mother. What is the matter?
Nurse.   Look, look! O heavy day!
Mother. O me, O me! My child, my only life!
Revive, look up, or I will die with thee!   20
Help, help! Call help.

Enter Father.

Father. For shame, bring Juliet forth; her lord is come.
Nurse. She's dead, deceased; she's dead, alack the day!
Mother. Alack the day, she's dead, she's dead, she's dead!
Capulet. Ha! let me see her. Out alas! she's cold,   25
    Her blood is settled, and her joints are stiff;
    Life and these lips have long been separated.

4 *pennyworths* small portions 6 *set . . . rest* i.e. made his firm decision
(from primero, a card game) 12 *down* back to bed 15 *weraday* welladay,
alas 16 *aqua vitae* alcoholic spirits

Death lies on her like an untimely frost
Upon the sweetest flower of all the field.
Nurse. O lamentable day!
30 *Mother.*   O woeful time!
Capulet. Death, that hath ta'en her hence to make me wail,
Ties up my tongue and will not let me speak.

*Enter Friar [Laurence] and the County [Paris, with
Musicians].*

Friar. Come, is the bride ready to go to church?
Capulet. Ready to go, but never to return.
35 O son, the night before thy wedding day
Hath Death lain with thy wife. There she lies,
Flower as she was, deflowerèd by him.
Death is my son-in-law, Death is my heir;
My daughter he hath wedded. I will die
40 And leave him all. Life, living, all is Death's.
Paris. Have I thought long to see this morning's face,
And doth it give me such a sight as this?
Mother. Accursed, unhappy, wretched, hateful day!
Most miserable hour that e'er time saw
45 In lasting labor of his pilgrimage!
But one, poor one, one poor and loving child,
But one thing to rejoice and solace in,
And cruel Death hath catched it from my sight.
Nurse. O woe! O woeful, woeful, woeful day!
50 Most lamentable day, most woeful day
That ever ever I did yet behold!
O day, O day, O day! O hateful day!
Never was seen so black a day as this.
O woeful day! O woeful day!
55 *Paris.* Beguiled, divorcèd, wrongèd, spited, slain!

45 *lasting labor* continuous toil   46 *But one* (cf. III, v, 166)

Most detestable Death, by thee beguiled,
By cruel cruel thee quite overthrown.
O love! O life! not life, but love in death!
Capulet. Despised, distressèd, hated, martyred, killed!
Uncomfortable time, why cam'st thou now 60
To murder, murder our solemnity?
O child, O child! my soul, and not my child!
Dead art thou — alack, my child is dead,
And with my child my joys are burièd!
Friar. Peace, ho, for shame! Confusion's cure lives not 65
In these confusions. Heaven and yourself
Had part in this fair maid — now heaven hath all,
And all the better is it for the maid.
Your part in her you could not keep from death,
But heaven keeps his part in eternal life. 70
The most you sought was her promotion,
For 'twas your heaven she should be advanced;
And weep ye now, seeing she is advanced
Above the clouds, as high as heaven itself?
O, in this love, you love your child so ill 75
That you run mad, seeing that she is well.
She's not well married that lives married long,
But she's best married that dies married young.
Dry up your tears and stick your rosemary
On this fair corse, and, as the custom is, 80
In all her best array bear her to church;
For though fond nature bids us all lament,
Yet nature's tears are reason's merriment.
Capulet. All things that we ordainèd festival

---

61 *To murder . . . solemnity* to spoil our ceremony 69 *Your part* her mortal
body, generated by her parents 70 *his part* her immortal soul, created
directly by God 79 *rosemary* plant symbolizing remembrance 82 *fond
nature* foolish human nature 83 *merriment* cause for optimism

85   Turn from their office to black funeral —
      Our instruments to melancholy bells,
      Our wedding cheer to a sad burial feast;
      Our solemn hymns to sullen dirges change;
      Our bridal flowers serve for a buried corse;
90   And all things change them to the contrary.
     Friar. Sir, go you in; and, madam, go with him;
      And go, Sir Paris. Every one prepare
      To follow this fair corse unto her grave.
      The heavens do low'r upon you for some ill;
95   Move them no more by crossing their high will.
        Exeunt [casting rosemary on her and shutting the curtains].
              Manet [the Nurse with Musicians].
   1. Musician. Faith, we may put up our pipes and be gone.
   Nurse. Honest good fellows, ah, put up, put up!
     For well you know this is a pitiful case.   *[Exit.]*
   1. Musician. Ay, by my troth, the case may be amended.

                  Enter Peter.

100 *Peter.* Musicians, O, musicians, 'Heart's ease,' 'Heart's ease'!
      O, an you will have me live, play 'Heart's ease.'
   1. Musician. Why 'Heart's ease'?
   Peter. O, musicians, because my heart itself plays 'My heart
     is full of woe.' O, play me some merry dump to comfort
105 me.
   1. Musician. Not a dump we! 'Tis no time to play now.
   Peter. You will not then?
   1. Musician. No.

94 *low'r* look angrily *ill* sin   95 s.d. *casting . . . curtains* (from Q1)   98 s.d.
(Q2 reads 'Exit omnes.')   99 *case* instrument case *amended* repaired
99 s.d. *Enter Peter* (Q2 has 'Enter Will Kemp,' the actor playing Peter's
role)   100, 103–4 *Heart's ease, My heart is full of woe* (old ballad tunes)
104 *dump* slow dance melody

Peter. I will then give it you soundly.

1. Musician. What will you give us?   110

Peter. No money, on my faith, but the gleek. I will give
   you the minstrel.

1. Musician. Then will I give you the serving-creature.

Peter. Then will I lay the serving-creature's dagger on your
   pate. I will carry no crotchets. I'll re you, I'll fa you. Do   115
   you note me?

1. Musician. An you re us and fa us, you note us.

2. Musician. Pray you put up your dagger, and put out
   your wit.

Peter. Then have at you with my wit! I will dry-beat you   120
   with an iron wit, and put up my iron dagger. Answer
   me like men.

>   'When griping grief the heart doth wound,
>   And doleful dumps the mind oppress,
>   Then music with her silver sound' —   125

Why 'silver sound'? Why 'music with her silver sound'?
What say you, Simon Catling?

1. Musician. Marry, sir, because silver hath a sweet sound.

Peter. Pretty! What say you, Hugh Rebeck?

2. Musician. I say 'silver sound' because musicians sound   130
   for silver.

Peter. Pretty too! What say you, James Soundpost?

3. Musician. Faith, I know not what to say.

Peter. O, I cry you mercy! you are the singer. I will say for

---

111 *gleek* mock   111–12 *give you* insultingly call you   115 *carry* put up
with   *crotchets* (1) whims (2) quarter notes in music   *re, fa* (musical notes)
118 *put out* display   120 *Then . . . wit* (added to preceding speech in Q2)
dry-beat thrash   123–25 (The second line is missing in Q2 but appears in
Q1. The song is from Richard Edwards' 'In Commendation of Music,'
in *The Paradise of Dainty Devices*, 1576.)   127 *Catling* (lutestring)   129
Rebeck (three-stringed fiddle)   132 *Soundpost* (wooden peg in a violin,
supporting the bridge)   134 *cry you mercy* beg your pardon

135   you. It is 'music with her silver sound' because musicians
      have no gold for sounding.
           'Then music with her silver sound
               With speedy help doth lend redress.'   *Exit*.
     1. Musician. What a pestilent knave is this same!
140 *2. Musician.* Hang him, Jack! Come, we'll in here, tarry
      for the mourners, and stay dinner.   *Exit [with others]*.

❦

V, i   *Enter Romeo.*

Romeo. If I may trust the flattering truth of sleep,
    My dreams presage some joyful news at hand.
    My bosom's lord sits lightly in his throne,
    And all this day an unaccustomed spirit
5   Lifts me above the ground with cheerful thoughts.
    I dreamt my lady came and found me dead
    (Strange dream that gives a dead man leave to think!)
    And breathed such life with kisses in my lips
    That I revived and was an emperor.
10 Ah me! how sweet is love itself possessed,
    When but love's shadows are so rich in joy!

        Enter Romeo's Man [Balthasar, booted].

    News from Verona! How now, Balthasar?
    Dost thou not bring me letters from the friar?
    How doth my lady? Is my father well?
15 How fares my Juliet? That I ask again,
    For nothing can be ill if she be well.

141 *stay* await V, i, 1 *flattering* favorable to me *truth of sleep* (cf. I, iv, 52)
3 *bosom's lord* heart 11 *shadows* dream-images

Man. Then she is well, and nothing can be ill.
    Her body sleeps in Capel's monument,
    And her immortal part with angels lives.
    I saw her laid low in her kindred's vault   20
    And presently took post to tell it you.
    O, pardon me for bringing these ill news,
    Since you did leave it for my office, sir.
Romeo. Is it e'en so? Then I defy you, stars!
    Thou knowest my lodging. Get me ink and paper   25
    And hire posthorses. I will hence to-night.
Man. I do beseech you, sir, have patience.
    Your looks are pale and wild and do import
    Some misadventure.
Romeo.   Tush, thou art deceived.
    Leave me and do the thing I bid thee do.   30
    Hast thou no letters to me from the friar?
Man. No, my good lord.
Romeo.   No matter. Get thee gone
    And hire those horses. I'll be with thee straight.

                                 Exit [Balthasar].

    Well, Juliet, I will lie with thee to-night.
    Let's see for means. O mischief, thou art swift   35
    To enter in the thoughts of desperate men!
    I do remember an apothecary,
    And hereabouts 'a dwells, which late I noted
    In tatt'red weeds, with overwhelming brows,
    Culling of simples. Meagre were his looks,   40
    Sharp misery had worn him to the bones;
    And in his needy shop a tortoise hung,
    An alligator stuffed, and other skins

21 *presently* at once *took post* hired posthorses 24 *stars* (cf. I, iv, 107)
28 *import* suggest 39 *weeds* garments *overwhelming* overhanging 40
simples herbs

Of ill-shaped fishes; and about his shelves
45   A beggarly account of empty boxes,
Green earthen pots, bladders, and musty seeds,
Remnants of packthread, and old cakes of roses
Were thinly scatterèd, to make up a show.
Noting this penury, to myself I said,
50   'An if a man did need a poison now
Whose sale is present death in Mantua,
Here lives a caitiff wretch would sell it him.'
O, this same thought did but forerun my need,
And this same needy man must sell it me.
55   As I remember, this should be the house.
Being holiday, the beggar's shop is shut.
What, ho! apothecary!

[Enter Apothecary.]

Apothecary.   Who calls so loud?
Romeo. Come hither, man. I see that thou art poor.
Hold, there is forty ducats. Let me have
60   A dram of poison, such soon-speeding gear
As will disperse itself through all the veins
That the life-weary taker may fall dead,
And that the trunk may be discharged of breath
As violently as hasty powder fired
65   Doth hurry from the fatal cannon's womb.
Apothecary. Such mortal drugs I have; but Mantua's law
Is death to any he that utters them.
Romeo. Art thou so bare and full of wretchedness
And fearest to die? Famine is in thy cheeks,
70   Need and oppression starveth in thy eyes,

45 *account* quantity   47 *cakes of roses* compressed rose petals, used for perfume   52 *caitiff* miserable   60 *gear* stuff   65 *womb* i.e. barrel   66 *mortal* deadly   67 *utters* gives out   70 *starveth* are revealed by the starved look

Contempt and beggary hangs upon thy back:
The world is not thy friend, nor the world's law;
The world affords no law to make thee rich;
Then be not poor, but break it and take this.
Apothecary. My poverty but not my will consents.   75
Romeo. I pay thy poverty and not thy will.
Apothecary. Put this in any liquid thing you will
And drink it off, and if you had the strength
Of twenty men, it would dispatch you straight.
Romeo. There is thy gold — worse poison to men's souls,   80
Doing more murder in this loathsome world,
Than these poor compounds that thou mayst not sell.
I sell thee poison; thou hast sold me none.
Farewell. Buy food and get thyself in flesh.
Come, cordial and not poison, go with me   85
To Juliet's grave; for there must I use thee.   *Exeunt.*

❀

Enter Friar John to Friar Laurence.   V, ii

John. Holy Franciscan friar, brother, ho!

Enter [Friar] Laurence.

Laurence. This same should be the voice of Friar John.
Welcome from Mantua. What says Romeo?
Or, if his mind be writ, give me his letter.
John. Going to find a barefoot brother out,   5
One of our order, to associate me
Here in this city visiting the sick,
And finding him, the searchers of the town,

V, ii, 5 *a barefoot brother* another friar 6 *associate* accompany 8 *searchers*
health officers

Suspecting that we both were in a house
10   Where the infectious pestilence did reign,
Sealed up the doors, and would not let us forth,
So that my speed to Mantua there was stayed.
Laurence. Who bare my letter, then, to Romeo?
John. I could not send it — here it is again —
15   Nor get a messenger to bring it thee,
So fearful were they of infection.
Laurence. Unhappy fortune! By my brotherhood,
The letter was not nice, but full of charge,
Of dear import; and the neglecting it
20   May do much danger. Friar John, go hence,
Get me an iron crow and bring it straight
Unto my cell.
John.   Brother, I'll go and bring it thee.   *Exit.*
Laurence. Now must I to the monument alone.
Within this three hours will fair Juliet wake.
25   She will beshrew me much that Romeo
Hath had no notice of these accidents;
But I will write again to Mantua,
And keep her at my cell till Romeo come —
Poor living corse, closed in a dead man's tomb!   *Exit.*

❧

V, iii   *Enter Paris and his Page [with flowers and sweet water].*

Paris. Give me thy torch, boy. Hence, and stand aloof.
Yet put it out, for I would not be seen.
Under yond yew tree lay thee all along,

---

10 *pestilence* plague   17 *brotherhood* order (Franciscans)   18 *nice* trivial
charge important matters   21 *crow* crowbar   25 *beshrew* reprove   26 *accidents* occurrences   V, iii, s.d. *with . . . water* (from Q1)   *sweet* perfumed
3 *all along* at full length

Holding thy ear close to the hollow ground.
So shall no foot upon the churchyard tread   5
(Being loose, unfirm, with digging up of graves)
But thou shalt hear it. Whistle then to me,
As signal that thou hearest something approach.
Give me those flowers. Do as I bid thee, go.
Page. *[aside]* I am almost afraid to stand alone   10
  Here in the churchyard; yet I will adventure.   *[Retires.]*
Paris. Sweet flower, with flowers thy bridal bed I strew
    (O woe! thy canopy is dust and stones)
  Which with sweet water nightly I will dew;
    Or, wanting that, with tears distilled by moans.   15
  The obsequies that I for thee will keep
  Nightly shall be to strew thy grave and weep.
                                          Whistle Boy.
  The boy gives warning something doth approach.
  What cursèd foot wanders this way to-night
  To cross my obsequies and true love's rite?   20
  What, with a torch? Muffle me, night, awhile. *[Retires.]*

*Enter Romeo, [and Balthasar with a torch, a mattock,
    and a crow of iron].*

Romeo. Give me that mattock and the wrenching iron.
  Hold, take this letter. Early in the morning
  See thou deliver it to my lord and father.
  Give me the light. Upon thy life I charge thee,   25
  Whate'er thou hearest or seest, stand all aloof
  And do not interrupt me in my course.
  Why I descend into this bed of death
  Is partly to behold my lady's face,
  But chiefly to take thence from her dead finger   30

20 *cross* interfere with 21 s.d. *and Balthasar . . . iron* (from Q1; Q2 reads
'Enter Romeo and Peter.') *mattock* pickaxe

A precious ring – a ring that I must use
In dear employment. Therefore hence, be gone.
But if thou, jealous, dost return to pry
In what I farther shall intend to do,

35   By heaven, I will tear thee joint by joint
And strew this hungry churchyard with thy limbs.
The time and my intents are savage-wild,
More fierce and more inexorable far
Than empty tigers or the roaring sea.

40 *Balthasar.* I will be gone, sir, and not trouble you.
   Romeo. So shalt thou show me friendship. Take thou that.
   Live, and be prosperous; and farewell, good fellow.
   Balthasar. *[aside]* For all this same, I'll hide me hereabout.
   His looks I fear, and his intents I doubt.   *[Retires.]*

45 *Romeo.* Thou detestable maw, thou womb of death,
   Gorged with the dearest morsel of the earth,
   Thus I enforce thy rotten jaws to open,
   And in despite I'll cram thee with more food.

                              [Romeo opens the tomb.]

   Paris. This is that banished haughty Montague

50   That murd'red my love's cousin – with which grief
   It is supposèd the fair creature died –
   And here is come to do some villainous shame
   To the dead bodies. I will apprehend him.
   Stop thy unhallowèd toil, vile Montague!

55   Can vengeance be pursued further than death?
   Condemnèd villain, I do apprehend thee.
   Obey, and go with me; for thou must die.
   Romeo. I must indeed; and therefore came I hither.

---

31 *A precious ring* (a false excuse to assure Balthasar's non-interference)
33 *jealous* curious, jealous of my privacy   41 *that* (a purse)   48 *in despite*
to spite you   48 S.D. (from Q1)   53 *apprehend* arrest

Good gentle youth, tempt not a desp'rate man.
Fly hence and leave me. Think upon these gone;   60
Let them affright thee. I beseech thee, youth,
Put not another sin upon my head
By urging me to fury. O, be gone!
By heaven, I love thee better than myself,
For I come hither armed against myself.   65
Stay not, be gone. Live, and hereafter say
A madman's mercy bid thee run away.
Paris. I do defy thy conjuration
    And apprehend thee for a felon here.
Romeo. Wilt thou provoke me? Then have at thee, boy!   70
                                        [They fight.]
Page. O Lord, they fight! I will go call the watch.
                                [Exit. Paris falls.]
Paris. O, I am slain! If thou be merciful,
    Open the tomb, lay me with Juliet.   *[Dies.]*
Romeo. In faith, I will. Let me peruse this face.
    Mercutio's kinsman, noble County Paris!   75
    What said my man when my betossèd soul
    Did not attend him as we rode? I think
    He told me Paris should have married Juliet.
    Said he not so? or did I dream it so?
    Or am I mad, hearing him talk of Juliet,   80
    To think it was so? O, give me thy hand,
    One writ with me in sour misfortune's book!
    I'll bury thee in a triumphant grave.
    A grave? O, no, a lanthorn, slaught'red youth,
    For here lies Juliet, and her beauty makes   85

---

60 *gone* dead 68 *conjuration* threatening appeal 74 *peruse* read, look at
77 *attend* pay attention to 84 *lanthorn* lantern (a many-windowed turret
room)

This vault a feasting presence full of light.
Death, lie thou there, by a dead man interred.

[Lays him in the tomb.]

How oft when men are at the point of death
Have they been merry! which their keepers call
90   A lightning before death. O, how may I
Call this a lightning? O my love! my wife!
Death, that hath sucked the honey of thy breath,
Hath had no power yet upon thy beauty.
Thou art not conquered. Beauty's ensign yet
95   Is crimson in thy lips and in thy cheeks,
And death's pale flag is not advancèd there.
Tybalt, liest thou there in thy bloody sheet?
O, what more favor can I do to thee
Than with that hand that cut thy youth in twain
100   To sunder his that was thine enemy?
Forgive me, cousin! Ah, dear Juliet,
Why art thou yet so fair? Shall I believe
That unsubstantial Death is amorous,
And that the lean abhorrèd monster keeps
105   Thee here in dark to be his paramour?
For fear of that I still will stay with thee
And never from this pallet of dim night
Depart again. Here, here will I remain
With worms that are thy chambermaids. O, here
110   Will I set up my everlasting rest

86 *presence* presence chamber   89 *keepers* jailers   90 *A lightning before
death* (a common phrase for the phenomenon described)   94 *ensign* banner
102 *Why . . . fair* (followed in Q2 by a superfluous 'I will believe,' evidently
another manuscript cancellation printed in error)   108 *again. Here* (Q2
prints between these words the following material, obviously cancelled in
the manuscript because it appears in substance later in the speech: 'come
lie thou in my arm. Here's to thy health, where e'er thou tumblest in.
O true Apothecary! Thy drugs are quick. Thus with a kiss I die. Depart
again.')   110 *set . . . rest* make my decision to stay forever (cf. IV, v, 6)

And shake the yoke of inauspicious stars
From this world-wearied flesh. Eyes, look your last!
Arms, take your last embrace! and, lips, O you
The doors of breath, seal with a righteous kiss
A dateless bargain to engrossing death!   115
Come, bitter conduct; come, unsavory guide!
Thou desperate pilot, now at once run on
The dashing rocks thy seasick weary bark!
Here's to my love! [Drinks.] O true apothecary!
Thy drugs are quick. Thus with a kiss I die.   [Falls.] 120

Enter Friar [Laurence], with lanthorn, crow, and spade.

Friar. Saint Francis be my speed! how oft to-night
  Have my old feet stumbled at graves! Who's there?
Balthasar. Here's one, a friend, and one that knows you well.
Friar. Bliss be upon you! Tell me, good my friend,
  What torch is yond that vainly lends his light   125
  To grubs and eyeless skulls? As I discern,
  It burneth in the Capels' monument.
Balthasar. It doth so, holy sir; and there's my master,
  One that you love.
Friar.   Who is it?
Balthasar.   Romeo.
Friar. How long hath he been there?
Balthasar.   Full half an hour.   130
Friar. Go with me to the vault.
Balthasar.   I dare not, sir.
  My master knows not but I am gone hence,

---

111 *inauspicious stars* (cf. V, i, 24) 115 *dateless* in perpetuity *engrossing*
taking everything 116 *conduct* guide, i.e. the poison 117 *pilot* i.e. Romeo's
soul 118 *bark* i.e. Romeo's body 119 *Here's to my love* (cf. IV, iii, 58)
121 *speed* aid 122 *stumbled at graves* (a bad omen)

139

And fearfully did menace me with death
If I did stay to look on his intents.
135 *Friar.* Stay then; I'll go alone. Fear comes upon me.
O, much I fear some ill unthrifty thing.
Balthasar. As I did sleep under this yew tree here,
I dreamt my master and another fought,
And that my master slew him.
Friar.   Romeo!
140 Alack, alack, what blood is this which stains
The stony entrance of this sepulchre?
What mean these masterless and gory swords
To lie discolored by this place of peace? *[Enters the tomb.]*
Romeo! O, pale! Who else? What, Paris too?
145 And steeped in blood? Ah, what an unkind hour
Is guilty of this lamentable chance!
The lady stirs.   *[Juliet rises.]*
Juliet. O comfortable friar! where is my lord?
I do remember well where I should be,
150 And there I am. Where is my Romeo?
Friar. I hear some noise. Lady, come from that nest
Of death, contagion, and unnatural sleep.
A greater power than we can contradict
Hath thwarted our intents. Come, come away.
155 Thy husband in thy bosom there lies dead;
And Paris too. Come, I'll dispose of thee
Among a sisterhood of holy nuns.
Stay not to question, for the watch is coming.
Come, go, good Juliet. I dare no longer stay.
160 *Juliet.* Go, get thee hence, for I will not away. *Exit [Friar].*
What's here? A cup, closed in my true love's hand?
Poison, I see, hath been his timeless end.

136 *unthrifty* unfortunate   148 *comfortable* comfort-giving   162 *timeless*
untimely

O churl! drunk all, and left no friendly drop
To help me after? I will kiss thy lips.
Haply some poison yet doth hang on them   165
To make me die with a restorative.   *[Kisses him.]*
Thy lips are warm!
Chief Watchman. [within] Lead, boy. Which way?
Juliet. Yea, noise? Then I'll be brief. O happy dagger!
                            [Snatches Romeo's dagger.]
This is thy sheath; there rust, and let me die.   170
                            [She stabs herself and falls.]

Enter [Paris's] Boy and Watch.

Boy. This is the place. There, where the torch doth burn.
Chief Watchman. The ground is bloody. Search about the
    churchyard.
Go, some of you; whoe'er you find attach.
                            [Exeunt some of the Watch.]
Pitiful sight! here lies the County slain;
And Juliet bleeding, warm, and newly dead,   175
Who here hath lain this two days burièd.
Go, tell the Prince; run to the Capulets;
Raise up the Montagues; some others search.
                            [Exeunt others of the Watch.]
We see the ground whereon these woes do lie,
But the true ground of all these piteous woes   180
We cannot without circumstance descry.

Enter [some of the Watch, with] Romeo's Man [Balthasar].

2. *Watchman.* Here's Romeo's man. We found him in the
    churchyard.

166 *restorative* i.e. restoring me to you   169 *happy* opportune   170 *rust*
(Q1 'rest')   180 *ground* basis   181 *circumstance* details

Chief Watchman. Hold him in safety till the Prince come
  hither.

Enter Friar [Laurence] and another Watchman.

3. Watchman. Here is a friar that trembles, sighs, and weeps.
185   We took this mattock and this spade from him
    As he was coming from this churchyard side.
Chief Watchman. A great suspicion! Stay the friar too.

Enter the Prince [and Attendants].

Prince. What misadventure is so early up,
    That calls our person from our morning rest?

Enter Capulet and his Wife [with others].

190 *Capulet.* What should it be, that is so shrieked abroad?
Wife. O the people in the street cry 'Romeo,'
    Some 'Juliet,' and some 'Paris'; and all run,
    With open outcry, toward our monument.
Prince. What fear is this which startles in your ears?
Chief Watchman. Sovereign, here lies the County Paris
195   slain;
    And Romeo dead; and Juliet, dead before,
    Warm and new killed.
Prince. Search, seek, and know how this foul murder comes.
Chief Watchman. Here is a friar, and slaughtered Romeo's
    man,
200   With instruments upon them fit to open
    These dead men's tombs.
Capulet. O heavens! O wife, look how our daughter bleeds!
    This dagger hath mista'en, for, lo, his house

189 s.d. *Enter . . . Wife* (in Q2 'Enter Capels' appears here, with the
present stage direction after l. 201)   203 *his house* its sheath

Is empty on the back of Montague,
And it missheathèd in my daughter's bosom!   205
Wife. O me! this sight of death is as a bell
That warns my old age to a sepulchre.

Enter Montague [and others].

Prince. Come, Montague; for thou art early up
To see thy son and heir more early down.
Montague. Alas, my liege, my wife is dead to-night!   210
Grief of my son's exile hath stopped her breath.
What further woe conspires against mine age?
Prince. Look, and thou shalt see.
Montague. O thou untaught! what manners is in this,
To press before thy father to a grave?   215
Prince. Seal up the mouth of outrage for a while,
Till we can clear these ambiguities
And know their spring, their head, their true descent;
And then will I be general of your woes
And lead you even to death. Meantime forbear,   220
And let mischance be slave to patience.
Bring forth the parties of suspicion.
Friar. I am the greatest, able to do least,
Yet most suspected, as the time and place
Doth make against me, of this direful murder;   225
And here I stand, both to impeach and purge
Myself condemnèd and myself excused.
Prince. Then say at once what thou dost know in this.
Friar. I will be brief, for my short date of breath
Is not so long as is a tedious tale.   230

207 *my old age* (she is only twenty-eight—I, iii, 72–73—but she feels old
and ready for death; cf. III, ii, 89)   216 *mouth of outrage* violent outcries
219 *general . . . woes* your leader in lamentation   220 *even to death* even
if grief kills us   226 *impeach and purge* accuse and exonerate   229 *date of
breath* life expectancy

143

Romeo, there dead, was husband to that Juliet;
And she, there dead, that Romeo's faithful wife.
I married them; and their stol'n marriage day
Was Tybalt's doomsday, whose untimely death
235 Banished the new-made bridegroom from this city;
For whom, and not for Tybalt, Juliet pined.
You, to remove that siege of grief from her,
Betrothed and would have married her perforce
To County Paris. Then comes she to me
240 And with wild looks bid me devise some mean
To rid her from this second marriage,
Or in my cell there would she kill herself.
Then gave I her (so tutored by my art)
A sleeping potion; which so took effect
245 As I intended, for it wrought on her
The form of death. Meantime I writ to Romeo
That he should hither come as this dire night
To help to take her from her borrowèd grave,
Being the time the potion's force should cease.
250 But he which bore my letter, Friar John,
Was stayed by accident, and yesternight
Returned my letter back. Then all alone
At the prefixèd hour of her waking
Came I to take her from her kindred's vault;
255 Meaning to keep her closely at my cell
Till I conveniently could send to Romeo.
But when I came, some minute ere the time
Of her awakening, here untimely lay
The noble Paris and true Romeo dead.
260 She wakes; and I entreated her come forth
And bear this work of heaven with patience;
But then a noise did scare me from the tomb,

238 *perforce* by force   247 *as* on   255 *closely* secretly

And she, too desperate, would not go with me,
But, as it seems, did violence on herself.
All this I know, and to the marriage   265
Her nurse is privy; and if aught in this
Miscarried by my fault, let my old life
Be sacrificed, some hour before his time,
Unto the rigor of severest law.
Prince. We still have known thee for a holy man.   270
　　Where's Romeo's man? What can he say in this?
Balthasar. I brought my master news of Juliet's death;
　　And then in post he came from Mantua
　　To this same place, to this same monument.
　　This letter he early bid me give his father,   275
　　And threat'ned me with death, going in the vault,
　　If I departed not and left him there.
Prince. Give me the letter. I will look on it.
　　Where is the County's page that raised the watch?
　　Sirrah, what made your master in this place?   280
Boy. He came with flowers to strew his lady's grave;
　　And bid me stand aloof, and so I did.
　　Anon comes one with light to ope the tomb;
　　And by and by my master drew on him;
　　And then I ran away to call the watch.   285
Prince. This letter doth make good the friar's words,
　　Their course of love, the tidings of her death;
　　And here he writes that he did buy a poison
　　Of a poor pothecary, and therewithal
　　Came to this vault to die, and lie with Juliet.   290
　　Where be these enemies? Capulet, Montague,
　　See what a scourge is laid upon your hate,
　　That heaven finds means to kill your joys with love.

266 *privy* in the secret   270 *still* always   280 *made* did   283 *Anon* soon
284 *by and by* almost at once   *drew* drew his sword   293 *with* by means of

And I, for winking at your discords too,
295 Have lost a brace of kinsmen. All are punished.
Capulet. O brother Montague, give me thy hand.
This is my daughter's jointure, for no more
Can I demand.
Montague. But I can give thee more;
For I will raise her statue in pure gold,
300 That whiles Verona by that name is known,
There shall no figure at such rate be set
As that of true and faithful Juliet.
Capulet. As rich shall Romeo's by his lady's lie —
Poor sacrifices of our enmity!
305 *Prince.* A glooming peace this morning with it brings.
The sun for sorrow will not show his head.
Go hence, to have more talk of these sad things;
Some shall be pardoned, and some punishèd;
For never was a story of more woe
310 Than this of Juliet and her Romeo.   *[Exeunt omnes.]*

294 *winking at* shutting my eyes to 297 *jointure* marriage portion 301
rate value 305 *glooming* cloudy, overcast

Supplementary Note

III, ii, 49 *Or those eyes' shot that makes the answer 'I'*

Almost every editor since Capell has accepted his emendation *shut* for *shot*, reading "Or those eyes shut that make(s) thee answer 'I' [Ay]." Our copy-text, Q2, reads: "Or those eyes shot, that makes thee answer I." This reading is retained by the later quartos and folios, except that *thee* is emended to *the* in F2, F3, and F4.

I have supplied the apostrophe which makes *eyes* a possessive. Since Q2 regularly omits the apostrophe, as in "eyes windows" (IV, i, 100), supplying it does no violence to the text. *Shot* becomes a noun instead of a past participle. A usage similar to this appears in *Cymbeline*, I, i, 89–90, when Imogen says, "And I shall here abide the hourly shot / Of angry eyes."

If we interpret the passage as emended by Capell, Juliet refers to Romeo's eyes closed in death; or else she refers to the Nurse's eyes which, if shut, will indicate *ay*. If, as I think, the Nurse's eyes are meant, *shot* is the more logical reading. Juliet is studying the Nurse's face and may receive her answer from the Nurse's voice or, failing that, from the Nurse's eyes. Either form of affirmative, the spoken *ay* or the revelatory eye-glance (*eyes' shot*), will slay Juliet, who feels that her life is bound up with that of Romeo. As the eye-glance of the cockatrice (basilisk) darts death, so will the spoken *ay* or the eye-glance of the Nurse. This implies no malice on the part of the Nurse, since it is her message which may be fatal to Juliet.

Involved here is the Elizabethan theory of vision, or the act of seeing. It was believed that the eye darted forth a stream of very fine particles which pierced or fastened upon the beheld object and then relayed impulses back to the sender. The arrow was the appropriate image for such an eye-glance. Thus, Juliet promises her mother to look at Paris, "But no more deep will I endart mine eye" than her mother wishes (I, iii, 98). Such imagery is very common in the works of Shakespeare and his contemporaries.

If one retains *thee* as the correct reading, Juliet's meaning is as follows: "I am not myself if there be such a spoken *ay* or if there

147

be your eye-glance that forces you to answer 'Ay.' " This makes sense after a fashion, but I have adopted the less tortuous reading of the later folios, changing *thee* to *the*. Juliet's meaning then becomes: "I am not myself if there be such a spoken *ay* or if there be your eye-glance that forms the answer 'Ay.' "

In support of the interpretation here given, we may notice that Mercutio pictures Romeo as being "dead," pierced by vision and by sound: "stabbed with a white wench's black eye; run through the ear with a love song" (II, iv, 13–15). So it is with Juliet. The spoken *ay* of the Nurse may slay her through the ear as effectively as the visual eye-dart of the cockatrice. Likewise, the Nurse's "eyes' shot," if it reveals the unspoken *ay*, will kill visually as effectively as her voice would kill through the ear.

Textual Variants

The only departures from the copy-text (second quarto, 1599) are listed below, except for relineations, corrections of obvious typographical errors, added stage directions (in brackets), and the treatment of cancelled passages (explained in the notes). Variants in speech prefixes within a scene have been regularized without comment. All the listed readings have been adopted from the first quarto, 1597, except those marked 'Q3' (third quarto, 1609), 'Q4' (fourth quarto, n.d.), 'F1' (first folio, 1623), 'F2' (second folio, 1632), 'F4' (fourth folio, 1683), and 'Eds' (emendation, usually made quite early in the history of Shakespearean textual study and still generally accepted by modern editors). The accepted readings are followed by the rejected readings of the copy-text.

I, i, 21 *cruel* (Q4) civil 26 *in sense* sense 30 *comes two* comes 60 *swashing* (Q4) washing 118 *drave* (F1) drive 151 *sun* (Eds) same 175 *create* created 177 *well-seeming* well-seeing 188 *raised* made 190 *lovers'* loving 200 *Bid a sick* A sick *make* makes 201 *Ah* A 209 *unharmed* uncharmed 216 *makes* (Q4) make

I, ii, 14 *The earth* (Q4) Earth 32 *on more view* (Q4) one more view 70 *and Livia* Livia

I, iii, 66, 67 *honor* hour 99 *make it fly* make fly

I, iv, 39 *done* 'dum' 42 *Of this sir-reverence* Or save your reverence 45 *like lamps* lights lights 47 *five wits* fine wits 61 *spider's* (F1) spider 66 *maid* man 72 *O'er courtiers'* On courtiers 81 *dreams he* he dreams 113 *sail* suit

I, v, 18 *Ah ha* Ah 95 *ready* did ready

II, i, 10 *pronounce* 'prouaunt' *dove* day 12 *heir* her 38 *et cetera,* or

II, ii, 31 *pacing* puffing 41 *nor any other part* (omitted in Q2) 44 *name* word 83 *washed* (F2) washeth 99 *havior* behavior 101 *more cunning* coying 110 *circled* circle 153 *suit* (Q4) strife 163 *mine* (omitted in Q2) 168 *sweet* (F2) 'Neece' *At what* What 179 *her* his 189 *father's* friar's close

II, iii, 4 *fiery* burning 22 *sometime's* sometime 74 *ring yet* yet ringing 85 *She whom* Her

II, iv, 19 *I can tell you* (omitted in Q2) 28-29 *fantasticoes* fantasies 96 (spoken by Romeo in Q2) 97 (spoken by Mercutio

in Q2)   109 *for* (omitted in Q2)   187 *I warrant* (F2) Warrant
197 *Ah* (Eds) A

II, v, 26 *have I had* (F2) have I

III, i, 106 *soundly too. Your* (Eds) soundly, to your   120 *Alive*
'He gan'   122 *eyed* 'end'   145 *O husband* (Eds) O cousin, husband
164 *agile* aged   186 *hate's* hearts

III, ii, 9 *By* (F2) And by   21 *he* (Q4) I   49 *the* (F2) thee   51
determine of (F1) determine   76 *Dove-feathered* (Eds) Ravenous
dove-feathered   79 *damnèd* (F2) 'dimme'

III, iii, 15 *Hence* Here   52 *Thou* Then   117 *lives* (F4) lies   138
happy too happy   143 *misbehaved* 'mishavèd'   144 *pout'st upon*
(Eds) puts up   163 *is* sir

III, iv, 34 *very very* very

III, v, 13 *exhales* exhale   83 *pardon him* (F2) pardon   182 *trained*
'liand'

IV, i, 7 *talked* talk   45 *cure* care   46 *Ah* O   72 *slay* stay   83
chapless 'chapels'   85 *his shroud* (Q4) his   98 *breath* breast   100
wanny (Eds) many   116 *waking* (Q3) walking

IV, iii, 58 *Romeo . . . thee* Romeo, Romeo, Romeo, here's
drink, I drink to thee

IV, v, 41 *long* love   65 *cure* (Eds) care   81 *In all* And in   82
fond (F2) some   104 *full of woe* (Q4) full   129, 132 *Pretty* Prates

V, i, 15 *fares my* doth my Lady   24 *defy* deny   76 *pay* pray

V, iii, 3 *yew tree* young trees   68 *conjuration* 'commiration'
137 *yew* (Q3) young   190 *shrieked* (Eds) 'shrike'   209 *more early*
'now earling'   232 *that* that's

*Details of the
Pelican Shakespeare and
other Penguin books
follow.*

THE PELICAN SHAKESPEARE

GENERAL EDITOR: ALFRED HARBAGE

The series has been planned to present in an inexpensive format a thoroughly sound text. Each play is published as a separate volume, edited by a specialist.

Tragedies

Edited by Maynard Mack	ANTONY AND CLEOPATRA
Harry Levin	CORIOLANUS
Willard Farnham	HAMLET
S. F. Johnson	JULIUS CAESAR
Alfred Harbage	KING LEAR
Alfred Harbage	MACBETH
Gerald E. Bentley	OTHELLO
John E. Hankins	ROMEO AND JULIET

Comedies

Ralph Sargent	AS YOU LIKE IT
Alfred Harbage	LOVE'S LABOR'S LOST★
R. C. Bald	MEASURE FOR MEASURE
Brents Stirling	THE MERCHANT OF VENICE
Fredson T. Bowers	THE MERRY WIVES OF WINDSOR★
Madeleine Doran	A MIDSUMMER NIGHT'S DREAM
Josephine Waters Bennett	MUCH ADO ABOUT NOTHING
Richard Hosley	THE TAMING OF THE SHREW★
Northrop Frye	THE TEMPEST
Virgil Whitaker	TROILUS AND CRESSIDA
Charles Prouty	TWELFTH NIGHT
Baldwin Maxwell	THE WINTER'S TALE

Histories and Poems

M. A. Shaaber	HENRY IV, PART I
Allan Chester	HENRY IV, PART II
Louis B. Wright and V. Freund	HENRY V
Irving Ribner	KING JOHN★
Matthew Black	RICHARD II
G. Blakemore Evans	RICHARD III
Douglas Bush	THE SONNETS

★In preparation

PLAYS BY BERNARD SHAW

*The following plays are published
in Penguin editions. Each play has the
complete text and the
author's preface*

CHAUCER: THE CANTERBURY TALES

A Modern Version By
Nevill Coghill

This is the first English work to be included in the Penguin Classics series of modern translations. When it was published it was widely acclaimed as a means of bringing Chaucer to thousands of people who would never have read him otherwise. Reviewers were quick to realize that Mr Coghill, who is a fellow of Exeter College, Oxford, was the right person to have attempted the task.

Punch offered very high praise by saying ' . . . this translation will remain a beloved classic until the language changes again sufficiently to call for another renaissance'. *The Manchester Guardian* found that 'Mr Coghill has achieved his aim that his translation should be considered as a poem and not as a crib'. And the most enthusiastic welcome came from *The Times Educational Supplement* which said, 'Altogether Mr Coghill's achievement is remarkable. He has been almost consistently successful and his practice carries out his theory and intentions. The bland, humorous, observing, and courtly spirit that informs the original is somehow preserved in a different idiom'.

528 pages. $1.45

THE PELICAN HISTORY OF ENGLAND

While each volume is complete in itself, the whole series, edited by J. E. Morpurgo, has been planned to provide an intelligent and consecutive guide to the development of English society in all its aspects. The eight volumes are:

SPECIALLY WRITTEN FOR PENGUINS

THE GREEK MYTHS

Robert Graves

Not for over a century, since Smith's *Dictionary of Classical Mythology* first appeared, has the attempt been made to provide for the English reader a complete 'mythology,' in the sense of a retelling in modern terms of the Greek tales of gods and heroes. In the two volumes of this book Robert Graves, whose combination of classical scholarship and anthropological competence has already been so brilliantly demonstrated in *The White Goddess* and *Hercules, My Shipmate*, and his other novels, supplies the need. In nearly two hundred sections, it covers the Creation myths, the legends of the birth and lives of the great Olympians, the Theseus, Oedipus, and Heracles cycles, the Argonaut voyage, the tale of Troy, and much else.

All the scattered elements of each myth have been assembled into a harmonious narrative, which notes also many variants which may help to determine its ritual or historical meaning. Full references to the classical sources, and copious indexes, make the book as valuable to the scholar as to the general reader; and a full commentary to each myth explains and interprets the classical version in the light of to-day's archaeological and anthropological knowledge.

A508, A509

Two volumes: $1.45 each